POETRY BY JOHN UPDIKE

The Carpentered Hen and Other Tame Creatures (1958)
Telephone Poles and Other Poems (1963)
Midpoint and Other Poems (1969)
Tossing and Turning (1977)
Facing Nature (1985)
Collected Poems 1953–1993 (1993)
Americana and Other Poems (2001)
Endpoint and Other Poems (2009)

FOR CHILDREN

A Child's Calendar (1965)
A Helpful Alphabet of Friendly Objects (1995)

Selected Poems

John Updike

Selected Poems

Edited by Christopher Carduff
Introduction by Brad Leithauser

HAMISH HAMILTON
an imprint of
PENGUIN BOOKS

HAMISH HAMILTON

UK | USA | Canada | Ireland | Australia
India | New Zealand | South Africa

Hamish Hamilton is part of the Penguin Random House group of companies
whose addresses can be found at global.penguinrandomhouse.com.

First published in the United States of America by Alfred A. Knopf 2015
First published in Great Britain by Hamish Hamilton 2016
001

Printed in the United States of America

A CIP catalogue record for this book is available from the British Library

ISBN: 978–0–241–24939–0

www.greenpenguin.co.uk

Penguin Random House is committed to a sustainable future for our business, our readers and our planet. This book is made from Forest Stewardship Council® certified paper.

Acknowledgments

Thirty-six of the poems printed here, and eleven of the seventeen parts of the poem titled "Endpoint," first appeared in *The New Yorker.* Others appeared in *The American Poetry Review*, *The American Scholar*, *Antæus*, *The Atlantic*, *Bits*, *Boston University Journal*, *Bostonian*, *The Christian Century*, *Crazy Horse*, *DoubleTake*, *The Formalist*, *The Georgia Review*, *Grand Street*, *Harper's*, *The Harvard Bulletin*, *The Harvard Lampoon*, *Literary Imagination*, *Michigan Quarterly Review*, *New England Monthly*, *The New Republic*, *The New York Quarterly*, *The New York Review of Books*, *Ontario Review*, *Oxford American*, *The Paris Review*, *Partisan Review*, *Per Contra*, *Poetry*, *Saturday Review*, *Scientific American*, *Shenandoah*, *The Southern California Anthology*, *The Transatlantic Review*, *Van Gogh's Ear*, and *The Yale Review.*

"Shillington" first appeared in *Fifty Years of Progress, 1908–1958: Shillington, Pennsylvania,* a publication of Shillington's Fiftieth Anniversary General Committee. The following presses first printed certain of these poems as broadsides or in limited-edition chapbooks: The Adams House and Lowell House Printers (Cambridge, Massachusetts), Limberlost Press (Boise, Idaho), The Literary Renaissance (Louisville, Kentucky), Lord John Press (Northridge, California), and Palæmon Press (Winston-Salem, North Carolina).

Contents

Editor's Note

This is a personal selection from the poetry that John Updike wrote between 1953, when he was twenty-one, and 2008, when he was seventy-six. The poems are ordered by date of completion, as determined by manuscript evidence gathered from the John Updike Papers at Harvard's Houghton Library. The Index of Titles doubles as a ready reference for years of completion. Exact dates of composition and the publication history of each poem can be found in the Notes.

When Updike arranged the contents of his *Collected Poems 1953–1993*, he took pains to separate his poetry from his light verse, assigning the latter a secondary status and relegating it to a sort of appendix. "If a set of lines brought back to me something I actually saw or felt, it was not light verse," he wrote in a preface. "If it took its spark from language and stylized signifiers"—from a newspaper headline, say, or an exotic name or spelling—"it was." I have tried to honor this "principle of segregation" in making this selection, and to include only items that John Updike would have deemed poems. The contents are drawn not only from *Collected Poems* (1993), whose sheep-and-goats arrangement is unambiguous, but also from *Americana* (2001), *Endpoint* (2009), and other "unsegregated" sources. I have omitted not only light verse but also verse for children, poems in translation, found poems, and lines written for family birthdays and other private occasions.

I would like to thank Deborah Garrison of Knopf for inviting me to edit this book, and Brad Leithauser, William H. Pritchard, Martha Updike, and Geoff Wisner for helping me to choose its contents. If, however, the reader believes that a goat got through the gate—or regrets that a favorite sheep is missing from the fold—he should lay the blame wholly on me.

C.C.

Introduction

In one of John Updike's early stories, the narrator urges us to contemplate his dead grandmother's thimble. Moving through a dark house, heading downstairs, he upends a sewing basket left on the landing. The moment's dislocation encourages one of Updike's greatest strengths, his flair for simile and metaphor. Retrieving the thimble from the floor, briefly uncertain what it is, he describes it as a "stemless chalice of silver weighing a fraction of an ounce." The metaphor's religious overtones are brightly suited to his succeeding sensations: "The valves of time parted, and after an interval of years my grandmother was upon me again, and it seemed incumbent upon me, necessary and holy, to tell how once there had been a woman who now was no more, how she had been born and lived in a world that had ceased to exist." He is inviting us to partake in one of literature's mystical rites—to drink deep and slake our souls from a chalice smaller, lighter than a tulip.

Updike was still in his twenties when he wrote these words, which appear in a story that bore, I suppose, the lengthiest title of any piece of fiction he ever published: "The Blessed Man of Boston, My Grandmother's Thimble, and Fanning Island." The young writer had already received, or was soon to receive, a host of propitious honors: a *summa cum laude* undergraduate degree from Harvard; employment at *The New Yorker;* book publication in three different genres (novel, poetry, short stories); and a widespread critical recognition that he'd already become, and promised long to be, a decisive shaper of contemporary American literature.

By contrast, the woman whose life's lineaments he was urging on his readers was a figure of little worldly consequence: elderly, insular, and infirm. She was sketched closely from life, and the fictional thimble was an actual thimble. She was Katherine Ziemer Kramer Hoyer, Updike's maternal grandmother, with whom—along with his mother, his father, and his grandfather—he lived throughout his childhood, much of it in a century-old farmhouse in Plowville, Pennsylvania, outside Reading. Though financially strapped, it was a richly populous household for the rearing of an only child. It was also what might be called the House of His Life; though Updike wrote lovingly and knowingly about various homes and buildings throughout his career, this sandstone farmhouse (bought at his mother's insistence, over the objections of her husband and her son, who resented its isolation) became his soul's dwelling place.

There's something touching in the distance between the blazing young man, so clearly bound for international fame, and the obscure woman who "never to my knowledge went outside the boundaries of Pennsylvania," who "had no possessions," who never attended a movie, and whom he never saw reading a book. But there's something more touching still in the way that, since Updike's death, in January of 2009, the distance between them foreshortens. Updike wrote unforgettably well about dying (arguably, the most moving scene he ever created was the drowning of the infant in *Rabbit, Run*), and he often meditated profoundly on how death serves as a great equalizer. With the closing of his life, after his amazing delivery of some sixty-plus books over his seventy-six years, it turns out that his long, weighty shelf of books bears a spiritual resemblance to that small, flyaway thimble. The shelf speaks, in effect, of "how once there had been a man, a writer, who now was no more," who was born and lived "in a world that had ceased to exist, though its mementos were all about us."

And I can think of no better way to contemplate that vanished man than through his poetry. Verse entranced him from the outset. Updike dated his career as a professional writer from his first acceptance by *The New Yorker*, at the age of twenty-two, of a light-verse poem, "Duet, with Muffled Brake Drums." The experience was bookended, in the last months of his life, by his final great creative project, a blossoming of verse that sprouted from the cracked vase of his diagnosis of stage IV lung cancer. He received this news in November of 2008, and was dead two months later. It wasn't much time to polish a surpassingly poignant poem-sequence, but even while he was deeply ailing, his inspired productivity endured.

That final book of poems, *Endpoint*, carries a dedication to his wife of thirty years: "For Martha, who asked for one more book: / here it is, with all my love." The words capture the aura of happily answerable gratitude—of yearning to offer some artistic repayment for all of life's unreckonable bounties—that suffuses most of his work. He spoke once of a writing studio "where my only duty was to describe reality as it had come to me—to give the mundane its beautiful due." The man felt summoned.

Some writers retire, but it's impossible to imagine Updike forsaking his writer's desk. *Endpoint*'s valedictory poems pulsate with a deep, soon-to-be-thwarted wish to resume his labors. One is reminded of Hokusai, who on his deathbed, at the age of eighty-eight, was reported to have cried, "If only Heaven will give me another ten years . . . Just another five more years, then I could become a real painter." Updike seemed to feel that in his writing life he'd tapped into something exterior and inextinguishable; the task was still beckoning him forward, even as he was severed from it.

The body of his verse gives us a remarkably full autobiographical portrait. In this, he's somewhat unusual. American poetry in the twentieth century abounded in wonderful poets from whose collected poetry it would be hard to concoct even a sketchy biography: John Crowe Ransom, T. S. Eliot, Marianne Moore, Weldon Kees, Louise Bogan, Elizabeth Bishop, Randall Jarrell, Donald Justice. For such writers, we must turn to their letters or to literary biographies to satisfy our hunger for details about their daily and their inner lives. But in Updike's case, he is often most openly and freely himself in poetry. He comes to it with an assured ease, instinctively constellating his thinking in that reverse Heaven whose stars are black balls of type and whose sky is the unbroken field of whiteness between stanzas.

I'm tempted to call what he does naked poetry, not least because he so often focused on erotic and bodily functions. He wrote poems called "Fellatio" and "Squirrels Mating" and "Mouse Sex" and "Elderly Sex" and "Cunts" and "Two Cunts in Paris" and "Klimt and Schiele Confront the Cunt"; he wrote a poem about a memorable defecation ("The Beautiful Bowel Movement") and gave us a detailed account of a colonoscopy. You could say that he offered us his body. It's in his poetry that we learn which hand he relied upon to perform which intimate ministrations.

But the poems are naked in a broader sense. They typically come to us unmediated through any fictional presence. You feel that it's Updike himself (or perhaps John himself, since the poems foster, even between strangers, a companionable familiarity) who is addressing you. There's nothing in his oeuvre like Richard Wilbur's "The Mind-Reader" or Anthony Hecht's "The Venetian Vespers"—gorgeous poems channeled through a complex, contrived persona. Though Updike was autobiographical throughout various genres, in his fiction I'm often uncertain how much of any particular incident is drawn from life directly and how much from artifice. With his poems, though, you typically sense he's chronicling his day-to-day existence; for more than half a century, poetry served as a diaristic outlet. Some of the poems are as casual as Polaroid snapshots. Others have the apportioned stiffness of a studio portrait. But in the aggregate the poems present an album of himself more accurate and intimate and multifaceted than any similar-sized collection of his prose.

Still, the term "naked poetry" might misleadingly suggest an abandonment of formal constraints, whereas little of Updike's poetry was written in free verse. The form he found most congenial was the unrhymed, loosely iambic sonnet—a structure whose packet of approximately 140 syllables granted him room to traffic in syntactic complexity while allowing for the brevity of casual utterance. The earliest of his unrhymed sonnets was "Topsfield Fair," of 1967, and the last were composed on death's threshold, as he completed the title sequence to *Endpoint.*

As a fiction writer, Updike became far more venturesome over time. The young man who grounded his first four novels in his local corner of southeastern Pennsylvania wound up setting later books in four different continents. The poems, too, wandered farther afield as he went along; he gave us dispatches from Russia, Japan, Italy, Greece, India. But, regarded by another light, the poems became less exploratory. In his versification, Updike tended to innovate and divagate less over the years. Some of the early poems have quite eccentric shapes and look a little peculiar on the page ("Seven Stanzas at Easter," "Hoeing," "The Great Scarf of Birds," and, especially, "Midpoint"). Later poems have, visually, a more staid deportment. Some readers may see this evolution as unfortunate; others will view at it as an example of an author gradually locating the forms he found most hospitable and returning to them with increasing self-possession. In any event, his farewell to verse, *Endpoint*, was the summit of his poetry collections.

"Nature is never bored," Updike observes in *Endpoint*'s title poem. He goes on:

> and we whose lives
> are linearly pinned to these aloof,
> self-fascinated cycles can't complain,
> though aches and pains and even dreams a-crawl
> with wood lice of decay give pause to praise.

The striking word-choice here is "self-fascinated." This is a notion or an image that surfaces constantly, in both his poetry and his prose: the meticulous onlooker who could hardly be described as an interloper or a trespasser, since the autonomous body under consideration is oblivious of any surveillance. Updike was forever gazing down through the round-cornered window of an airplane, or a magnifying glass, or a microscope, noting and speculating about the lives below. He does something similar in his extraterrestrial journeys, as in "The Moons of Jupiter," which begins:

> Callisto, Ganymede, Europa, Io:
> these four, their twinkling spied by Galileo
> in his new-invented telescope, debunked
> the dogma of celestial spheres . . .

Updike plays cicerone in the succeeding stanzas, providing a guided excursion to each of the four moons. Not surprisingly, the tours turn out to be metaphorical forays, into the recesses of memory and appetite. Cold Callisto is a terrain

> of unforgiven wrongs and hurts preserved—
> the unjust parental slap, the sneering note
> passed hand to hand in elementary school,
> the sexual jibe confided between cool sheets,
> the bad review, the lightly administered snub.

On steamy, volcanic Io,

> the bulblike limbic brain, the mother's breast,
> the fear of death, the wish to kill, the itch
> to plunge and flee, the love of excrement,
> the running sore and appetitive mouth
> all find form . . .

What *is* surprising is the delight he takes in rendering with a geologist's precision his extra-planetary landscapes; Updike was distinctive among contemporary poets in the unforced ease with which he appropriated the nomenclature and the rigors of the scientific imagination. Here is a more naturalistic view of Io:

> Kilometers away,
> a melancholy puckered caldera
> erupts, and magma, gas, and crystals hurl
> toward outer space a smooth blue column that
> umbrellas overhead—some particles
> escaping Io's seething gravity.

And Callisto:

> Its surface underfoot is ancient ice,
> thus frozen firm four billion years ago
> and chipped and peppered since into a slurry
> of saturated cratering.

One is reminded of H. G. Wells, whose *The Time Machine* revels in unthinkably remote panoramas, and of the Polish science fiction writer Stanislaw Lem, who in *Solaris* beamed such bizarre planetary formations down the heavens' icy starways and whom Updike, in words applicable to himself, extolled for his "easy access to the scientific terminology where he is at home, and a poet."

Updike's fiction abounds in portraits of the scientific temperament: the botanist in *Couples* striving to untie the knotted carbon-string mysteries of photosynthesis; the computer scientist in *Roger's Version* who seeks a digital proof of the existence of God; the Hungarian with "an air of seeing beyond me" in "The Astronomer"; the paleontologist manqué in "The Man Who Loved Extinct Mammals." His scientific interests often crossed and blurred the border he kept between his "poems" and his "light verse." He divided and delimited them in his preface to *Collected Poems:*

> In making this collection, I wanted to distinguish my poems from my light verse. My principle of segregation has been that a poem derives from the real

(the given, the substantial) world and light verse from the man-made world of information—books, newspapers, words, signs.

Following this designation, he offered "poems" about a lunar eclipse, a limestone fossil, entropy, a malfunctioning computer, and "light verse" about a dwarf star, neutrinos, neoteny, and the synthetic polyester known as Terylene ("In Praise of $(C_{10}H_9O_5)_x$").

The critic Randall Jarrell once noted, "When you know Frost's poems, you know surprisingly well what the world seemed to one man." This strikes me as about as handsome a compliment as can be paid to any writer, and it could certainly be said of John Updike. You leave his poems (or his short stories, or his novels, or his essays) feeling that you've encountered someone in great intimacy and wholeness. And Updike's accomplishment looks all the more striking in that he created this subtending unity across at least five genres: novels, short stories, essays, poems, and light verse, though perhaps some of these categories call for further subdivision. In any case, it appears beyond argument that no other American writer has written successfully in a greater diversity of modes.

Updike's distinction between poetry and light verse informs the present collection. Its editor, Christopher Carduff, has sought to gather only what Updike would himself have considered poems—occasionally an iffy judgment, when contemplating uncollected or unpublished material, but mostly an unambiguous task.

Stray poems will doubtless turn up over time. But I suspect that the corpus is virtually intact, and that, given Updike's scrupulosity about dating his work and notating revisions, it is unlikely to undergo any radical overhaul. This is a good time to take stock.

With his early poems, there's a keen pleasure in contemplating the directions the poet took and also might plausibly have taken—where he actually went and what he forwent. There's always something a little rueful to any such investigation. As Updike memorably reminded us in "The Bulgarian Poetess," one of his Bech stories, "Actuality is a running impoverishment of possibility." As one wanders through his earlier poems, one keeps coming upon Roads Not Taken, potentially fruitful pathways that turned out to be cul-de-sacs. A poem like "Shillington," for instance, composed when Updike was twenty-six, has a charm reminiscent of Frost or Richard Wilbur:

> Returning, we find our snapshots inexact.
> Perhaps a condition of being alive
> Is that the clothes which, setting out, we packed
> With love no longer fit when we arrive.

Though quite dexterously done, this sort of foursquare, somewhat folksy writing, with its clean rhymes and mostly strict iambic pentameter, wasn't a direction Updike would pursue with any fervor. Something similar occurs in a very early poem where you find him rhyming "umbrella" and "ele" (inelegantly breaking "elegant" across two lines). Though he'd continue to dally with this sort of forcible, antic splicing in his light verse, you won't find much of it among what he classified as his poems, where he gradually took a more casual and collected tone. Likewise, there's something quite promising in the roly-poly rhyming and the rhythmic rollick of the early "Vermont," though no subsequent poem sounds much like it. It concludes:

> Hawks, professors,
> And summering ministers
> Roost on the mountainsides of poverty
> And sniff the poetry,
>
> And every year
> The big black bear,
> Slavering through the woods with scrolling mouth,
> Comes further south.

A number of poems in his last book seem to extend a comradely wave to his earliest creations—a sort of Road Returned To. *Endpoint* offers a tribute to the singer Frankie Laine. The poem's first line is "The Stephens' Sweet Shop, 1949." We're in "an opium den of wooden booths," of "milkshakes thick as tar / and Coca-Cola conjured from syrup and fizz." Or you might say we're back in Mae's Luncheonette, the site of "Ex–Basketball Player," one of Updike's earliest poems (written when he was twenty-two) and a poetic prefiguring of his best-known prose creation: Harry Angstrom of the Rabbit tetralogy. "Ex–Basketball Player" gives us another breed of rabbit, this one named Flick, who is a master of the luncheonette's pinball machine. He ignores Mae, the proprietor, having an eye instead for an audience whose sweetness has turned cloying:

> Flick seldom says a word to Mae, just nods
> Beyond her face toward bright applauding tiers
> Of Necco Wafers, Nibs, and Juju Beads.

We have a further return to the sweet shop in one of my favorite poems in *Endpoint*, the disarmingly whimsical "Her Coy Lover Sings Out." It's an homage—not Updike's first—to Doris Day, for whom he fell hard in his teens and carried a torch till the end of his days. The poem is a modest construction, a paper airplane sent winging across that all-but-unbridgeable chasm that separates fandom from stardom. Here's the first stanza:

Doris, ever since 1945,
when I was all of thirteen and you a mere twenty-one,
and "Sentimental Journey" came winging
out of the juke box at the sweet shop,
your voice piercing me like a silver arrow,
I knew you were sexy.

And here's the fifth and last stanza, by which time most of the poem's silliness has bled away, leaving behind something poignant and measured:

Still, I'm not quite ready
for you to breathe the air that I breathe.
I huff going upstairs as it is.
Give me space to get over the *idea* of you—
the thrilling silver voice,
the gigantic silver screen. Go
easy on me. *Cara*, let's take our time.

As his title makes clear, Updike is having some fun with another coy lover, Andrew Marvell's. In "To His Coy Mistress," Marvell begs his beloved to forgo courtship's dilatory flirtations: "Now let us sport us while we may, / And now, like amorous birds of prey, / Rather at once our time devour . . ." Updike, by contrast, asks that everything be slowed down. We enter a world without hurry—a notion that haunted his last years. His poem's final line also echoes the conclusion of what I think of as his last great story, "The Walk with Elizanne," from *My Father's Tears:*

> David felt as he had when, his one weekend at the Jersey Shore the past summer, a wave carrying his surfing body broke too early and was about to throw him forward, down into the hard sand. "I want to hear it all," he told Elizanne. "We have t-tons of time."

But something still more interesting is going on here. I've rarely felt so strong a sense, in reading any poem, of a completely balanced dual audience. Love poems typically branch into two categories. There are those that feel ultimately intended for the loved one's ears, rendering the reader a somewhat superfluous outsider. (T. S. Eliot, in "A Dedication to My Wife," teases this notion: "These are private words addressed to you in public.") And there are those aimed at a broader audience, in which case the poet likely preens a bit, making a fine exhibition of his unparalleled passions. In recounting his crush on Doris Day, Updike is doing both. You feel he's showing off for us, letting us know what an irresistibly charming lover he can be. But you likewise, and equally, sense that he really is addressing Miss Day, with an adolescent's aching wishfulness that he has somehow managed to preserve, as something worth cherishing, across two-thirds of a century.

One of my favorite moments in Updike's fiction is, like so much in *Endpoint*, a hospital insight. It's found in *Rabbit at Rest.* After heart surgery, Harry Angstrom sprawls in a recovery bed, contemplating a row of old buildings across the way, and once again, as with Grandma's thimble, the valves of time open:

> Lying there these days, Harry thinks fondly of those dead bricklayers who bothered to vary their rows at the top of the three buildings across the street with such festive patterns of recess and protrusion, diagonal and upright, casting shadows in different ways at different times of the day, these men of another century up on their scaffold . . .

The passage is quintessential Updike in its hunger to prise out the idiosyncratic moment, the human story, from a surface that might initially appear remote and inhospitable and bland. It also attests to his fascination with every sort of work, especially visible, manual labor. Whether it's Joey Robinson in *Of the Farm* so lavishly choreographing the mowing of a field by tractor; or Harry Angstrom in *Rabbit Redux* operating a linotype machine; or Hummel's clanging garage in *The Centaur;* or the gunsmith in "The Gun Shop" with hands "battered and nicked and so long in touch with greased machinery that they had blackened flatnesses like worn parts"—Updike was forever eulogizing the virtues of tactile toil.

It's a trait shared with his friend L. E. Sissman, who once wrote a poem called "Work: A Sermon." Given the title, you might suppose irony was to follow, but instead we have a paean:

> Work, sisters and
> Brothers, not for riches or a land
> Of glory, but to write our testament
> Of love upon the day we seize.

Among contemporary poets, Sissman was Updike's closest sibling.* Contemplating his ill-fated friend, who developed cancer in his thirties and died at the age of forty-eight,

* Updike and Sissman—as poets, they make a curious pair of insiders/outsiders. On the one hand, both were warmly embraced by Howard Moss and Peter Davison, the longtime poetry editors of, respectively, *The New Yorker* and *The Atlantic,* which guaranteed their verse a mass readership. On the other hand, they were largely ignored by the rest of the American poetry establishment, which rarely looked to them when compiling anthologies or awarding prizes. The two men shared, among much else, a fascination with the dailiness of late-twentieth-century middle-class life, including its merchandise and merchandising. (Sissman made his living as an adman.) This and the prosy inclusiveness of their work often put them at

Updike observed that his "outburst of autobiographical verse, mostly blank, powered by the nearness of his death and a prodigious festive way with the English language, was to me the most impressive event in poetry in the 1960s." (Updike may have suffered a few premonitory shivers in writing those words, which so aptly foreshadow his own experience, decades later, when completing "Endpoint" under a death sentence.)

Hard, honest work will always be associated with Updike, chiefly for the unbroken way he turned out so much lucid and lively prose over the decades. The wonder of it is how little of his prose or poetry feels workaday, how much feels spirited and effervescent; this particular workhorse loved to caper. Praising Nabokov, Updike once spoke of how his sentences embrace the "body of a moment" with the "crunch of a superb adjective"—one of those occasions, common in his criticism, when the praise he offers reflects back on himself: you admire his word-choice even as he's praising another's word-choices. Updike made it look so easy, concealing all the struggling that went into selecting the right adjective, noun, verb. If a concordance of his complete works were to be assembled—an immense undertaking, but no daunting task for a computer—it would reveal a more far-reaching vocabulary (drawing on the nomenclature of biology, astronomy, architecture, painting, music, mathematics, sports, fashion, as well as contemporary and outdated slang, and a generous swath of Victorian verbal furbelows) than that employed by nearly all of his contemporaries. He put the dictionary through its paces.

But a still more impressive aspect to his labors is something that, I'm happy to say, might not be immediately amenable to computer analysis: the flexible uses to which he put those least glamorous parts of speech, prepositions and conjunctions. Over them he seemed to wield an instinctive, athletic mastery, encouraging him to create an elaborate sentence architecture that was tensile and yet delicate. Time and again, he managed to slip smoothly and unsnagged through the grammarian's dense thickets of coordinating, subordinating, and correlative conjunctions. They were the little fulcra upon which his long sentences could shift their direction and weight in such unexpected, magnificent ways. Like any writer, he had his tics and his crutches, but in total he exhibited an almost astonishing ability to listen to the complex demands of what he wanted to say and devise for it a suitable linguistic structure, one that suffered remarkably little loss of nuance and brightness in the conversion from idea to implementation. Physicists have a non-technical-sounding technical term, waste heat, to describe an unwanted, inevitable entropic by-product—like the warmth emitted by a refrigerator. Some of Updike's sentences feel like physics-defying miracles of efficiency.

To my mind, he was the twentieth-century American writer who created the greatest number of zingers—sentences you want to place check marks beside, and extract from their surroundings to scrutinize as separate entities, and eventually perhaps tinker

---

cross-purposes with a strong current in American poetry that saw itself as consciously anti-materialistic, in pursuit of sparseness and a renunciatory spiritualism.

with, in an attempt to understand better why they perform so well. (In this, he was to the twentieth century what Henry James was to the nineteenth.)

One such sentence comprises the envoi in Updike's penultimate volume of verse, *Americana and Other Poems*. Its title is "A Sound Heard Early on the Morning of Christ's Nativity," with Updike again alluding to a canonical figure, in this case John Milton, whose "On the Morning of Christ's Nativity" is sometimes seen as his first masterpiece. If the poem is harking back to Milton, it's also another meditation about physical labor. On a dark and despondent morning, a manger's glow unites both the outdoor deliveryman and the indoor wordsmith. Everything hangs together. And a noun left dangling at the end of line 4 clasps its verb at the start of the sonnet's final line:

> The thump of the newspaper on the porch
> on Christmas Day, in the dark before dawn
> yet after Santa Claus has left his gifts:
> the real world reawakens; some poor devil,
> ill-paid to tear himself from bed and face
> the starless cold, the Godforsaken gloom,
> and start his car, and at the depot pack
> his bundle in the seat beside his own
> and launch himself upon his route, the news
> affording itself no holiday, not even
> this anniversary of Jesus' birth,
> when angels, shepherds, oxen, Mary, all
> surrendered sleep to the divine design,
> has brought to us glad tidings, and we stir.

It was only one year after Updike's death that the chairman of the board of the nation's leading newspaper conceded, "We will stop printing *The New York Times* sometime in the future." Paper isn't in the paper's future. Its destiny is digital, and Updike's poem, however unwittingly, gathers to itself an elegiac air. Once a symbol of the up-to-the-minute, our morning newspapers become, in the fullness of time, objects as quaint as a manger; their percussive thump upon a concrete front porch joins the musical cooing of the passenger pigeon.

Reflecting on his grandmother's thimble, the young Updike saw that in meditating upon the loss of any beloved figure we wind up, inescapably, lamenting the loss of "a world that had ceased to exist." When we mourn Updike's passing, we mourn an America stretching from the Great Depression through the Second World War, across the turbulence of the sixties and seventies, through the technological explosions of the eighties and nineties, and into the first bedazzling decade of a new millennium. The breadth of his appetite for that world was remarkably capacious: he savored its slang, its gizmos, its pop songs and advertisements, its push and welter, its turnarounds, its exploratory carnality, its computational wizardry, its bumbling altruism, its triumphs, its ever-altering landscape. He embraced all of it in prose, embraced it in poetry. No other writer of his time captured so much of this passing pageant. And that he did so with brio and delight and nimbleness is another reason to celebrate our noble celebrant.

Brad Leithauser
Amherst, Massachusetts
2014

Selected Poems

WHY THE TELEPHONE WIRES DIP AND THE POLES ARE CRACKED AND CROOKED

The old men say
young men in gray
hung this thread across our plains
acres and acres ago.

But we, the enlightened, know
in point of fact it's what remains
of the flight of a marvellous crow
no one saw:
each pole, a caw.

COMING INTO NEW YORK

After Providence, Connecticut—
the green defiant landscape, unrelieved
except by ordered cities, smart and smug,
in spirit villages, too full of life
to be so called, too small to seem sincere.
And then like Death it comes upon us:
the plain of steaming trash, the tinge of brown
that colors now the trees and grass as though
exposed to rays sent from the core of heat—
these are the signs we see in retrospect.
But we look up amazed and wonder that
the green is gone out of our window, that
horizon on all sides is segmented
into so many tiny lines that we
mistake it for the profile of a wooded
hill against the sky, or that as far
as mind can go are buildings, paving, streets.
The tall ones rise into the mist like gods
serene and watchful, yet we fear, for we
have witnessed from this train the struggle to
complexity: the leaf has turned to stone.

EX–BASKETBALL PLAYER

Pearl Avenue runs past the high-school lot,
Bends with the trolley tracks, and stops, cut off
Before it has a chance to go two blocks,
At Colonel McComsky Plaza. Berth's Garage
Is on the corner facing west, and there,
Most days, you'll find Flick Webb, who helps Berth out.

Flick stands tall among the idiot pumps—
Five on a side, the old bubble-head style,
Their rubber elbows hanging loose and low.
One's nostrils are two S's, and his eyes
An E and O. And one is squat, without
A head at all—more of a football type.

Once Flick played for the high-school team, the Wizards.
He was good: in fact, the best. In '46
He bucketed three hundred ninety points,
A county record still. The ball loved Flick.
I saw him rack up thirty-eight or forty
In one home game. His hands were like wild birds.

He never learned a trade, he just sells gas,
Checks oil, and changes flats. Once in a while,
As a gag, he dribbles an inner tube,
But most of us remember anyway.
His hands are fine and nervous on the lug wrench.
It makes no difference to the lug wrench, though.

Off work, he hangs around Mae's Luncheonette.
Grease-gray and kind of coiled, he plays pinball,
Smokes those thin cigars, nurses lemon phosphates.
Flick seldom says a word to Mae, just nods
Beyond her face toward bright applauding tiers
Of Necco Wafers, Nibs, and Juju Beads.

SUNFLOWER

Sunflower, of flowers
the most lonely,
yardstick of hours,
long-term stander
in empty spaces,
shunner of bowers,
indolent bender
seldom, in only
the sharpest of showers:
tell us, why
is it your face is
a snarl of jet swirls
and gold arrows, a burning
old lion face high
in a cornflower sky,
yet by turning
your head, we find
you wear a girl's
bonnet behind?

BURNING TRASH

At night—the light turned off, the filament
Unburdened of its atom-eating charge,
His wife asleep, her breathing dipping low
To touch a swampy source—he thought of death.
Her father's hilltop home allowed him time
To sense the nothing standing like a sheet
Of speckless glass behind his human future.
He had two comforts he could see, just two.

One was the cheerful fullness of most things:
Plump stones and clouds, expectant pods, the soil
Offering up pressure to his knees and hands.
The other was burning the trash each day.
He liked the heat, the imitation danger,
And the way, as he tossed in used-up news,
String, napkins, envelopes, and paper cups,
Hypnotic tongues of order intervened.

TAO IN THE YANKEE STADIUM BLEACHERS

(*Having Taken Along to the Ball Game*
Arthur Waley's Three Ways of Thought in Ancient China)

Distance brings proportion. From here
the populated tiers
as much as players seem part of the show:
a constructed stage beast, three folds of Dante's rose,
or a Chinese military hat
cunningly chased with bodies.
"Falling from his chariot, a drunk man is unhurt
because his soul is intact. Not knowing his fall,
he is unastonished, he is invulnerable."
So, too, the "pure man"—"pure"
in the sense of undisturbed water.

"It is not necessary to seek out
a wasteland, swamp, or thicket."
The opposing pitcher's pertinent hesitations,
the sky, this meadow, Mantle's thick baked neck,
the old men who in the changing rosters see
a personal mutability,
green slats, wet stone are all to me
as when an emperor commands
a performance with a gesture of his eyes.

"No king on his throne has the joy of the dead,"
the skull told Chuang-tzu.
The thought of death is peppermint to you
when games begin with patriotic song
and a democratic sun beats broadly down.
The Inner Journey seems unjudgeably long
when small boys purchase cups of ice
and, distant as a paradise,
experts, passionate and deft,
hold motionless while Berra flies to left.

SHILLINGTON

The vacant lots are occupied, the woods
Diminish, Slate Hill sinks beneath its crown
Of solvent homes, and marketable goods
On all sides crowd the good remembered town.

Returning, we find our snapshots inexact.
Perhaps a condition of being alive
Is that the clothes which, setting out, we packed
With love no longer fit when we arrive.

Yet sights that limited our truth were strange
To older eyes; the town that we have lost
Is being found by hands that still arrange
Horse-chestnut heaps and fingerpaint on frost.

Time shades these alleys; every pavement crack
Is mapped somewhere. A solemn concrete ball,
On the gatepost of a sold house, brings back
A waist leaning against a buckling wall.

The gutter-fires smoke, their burning done
Except for, fanned within, an orange feather;
We have one home, the first, and leave that one.
The having and leaving go on together.

MOBILE OF BIRDS

There is something
in their planetary weave that is comforting.

The polycentric orbits, elliptical
with mutual motion,
random as nature, and yet, above all,
calculable, recall
those old Ptolemaic heavens small
enough for the Byzantine Trinity,
        Plato's Ideals,
        formal devotion,
seven levels of bliss, and numberless wheels
of omen, balanced occultly.

                                        A small bird
at an arc's extremity
adequately weights
his larger mates'
compounded mass: absurd
but actual—there he floats!

Persisting through a doorway, shadow-casting light
        dissolves on the wall
        the mobile's threads
and turns its spatial conversation
dialectical. Silhouettes,
projections of identities,
merge and part and reunite
in shapely syntheses—
                                an illusion,
for the birds on their perches of fine wire avoid collusion
and are twirled
alone in their suspenseful world.

TELEPHONE POLES

They have been with us a long time.
They will outlast the elms.
Our eyes, like the eyes of a savage sieving the trees
In his search for game,
Run through them. They blend along small-town streets
Like a race of giants that have faded into mere mythology.
Our eyes, washed clean of belief,
Lift incredulous to their fearsome crowns of bolts, trusses, struts, nuts, insulators,
  and such
Barnacles as compose
These weathered encrustations of electrical debris—
Each a Gorgon's head, which, seized right,
Could stun us to stone.

Yet they are ours. We made them.
See here, where the cleats of linemen
Have roughened a second bark
Onto the bald trunk. And these spikes
Have been driven sideways at intervals handy for human legs.
The Nature of our construction is in every way
A better fit than the Nature it displaces.
What other tree can you climb where the birds' twitter,
Unscrambled, is English? True, their thin shade is negligible,
But then again there is not that tragic autumnal
Casting-off of leaves to outface annually.
These giants are more constant than evergreens
By being never green.

MODIGLIANI'S DEATH MASK

Fogg Museum, Cambridge

The shell of a doll's head,
It stares askew, lopsided in death,
With nervous lips, a dirty tan,
And no bigger than my hand.
Could the man have been that small?
Or is life, like rapid motion,
An enlarging illusion?
Ringed, Italianly, with ivy,
The mask makes an effect of litter,
Preserved inside its glass case like
An oddly favored grapefruit rind.

SEAGULLS

A gull, up close,
looks surprisingly stuffed.
His fluffy chest seems filled
with an inexpensive taxidermist's material
rather lumpily inserted. The legs,
unbent, are childish crayon strokes—
too simple to be workable.
And even the feather-markings,
whose intricate symmetry is the usual glory of birds,
are in the gull slovenly,
as if God makes too many
to make them very well.

Are they intelligent?
We imagine so, because they are ugly.
The sardonic one-eyed profile, slightly cross,
the narrow, ectomorphic head, badly combed,
the wide and nervous and well-muscled rump
all suggest deskwork: shipping rates
by day, Schopenhauer
by night, and endless coffee.

At that hour on the beach
when the flies begin biting in the renewed coolness
and the backsliding skin of the after-surf
reflects a pink shimmer before being blotted,
the gulls stand around in the dimpled sand
like those melancholy European crowds
that gather in cobbled public squares in the wake
of assassinations and invasions,
heads cocked to hear the latest radio reports.

It is also this hour when plump young couples
walk down to the water, bumping together,
and stand thigh-deep in the rhythmic glass.
Then they walk back toward the car,
tugging as if at a secret between them,

but which neither quite knows—
walk capricious paths through the scattering gulls,
as in some mythologies
beautiful gods stroll unconcerned
among our mortal apprehensions.

SEVEN STANZAS AT EASTER

Make no mistake: if He rose at all
it was as His body;
if the cells' dissolution did not reverse, the molecules reknit, the amino acids rekindle,
the Church will fall.

It was not as the flowers,
each soft spring recurrent;
it was not as His Spirit in the mouths and fuddled eyes of the eleven apostles;
it was as His flesh: ours.

The same hinged thumbs and toes,
the same valved heart
that—pierced—died, withered, paused, and then regathered out of enduring Might
new strength to enclose.

Let us not mock God with metaphor,
analogy, sidestepping, transcendence,
making of the event a parable, a sign painted in the faded credulity of earlier ages:
let us walk through the door.

The stone is rolled back, not papier-mâché,
not a stone in a story,
but the vast rock of materiality that in the slow grinding of time will eclipse for each of us
the wide light of day.

And if we will have an angel at the tomb,
make it a real angel,
weighty with Max Planck's quanta, vivid with hair, opaque in the dawn light, robed in real linen
spun on a definite loom.

Let us not seek to make it less monstrous,
for our own convenience, our own sense of beauty,
lest, awakened in one unthinkable hour, we are embarrassed by the miracle,
and crushed by remonstrance.

B.W.I.

Under a priceless sun,
   Shanties and guava.
Beside an emerald sea,
   Coral and lava.

On the white dirt road,
   A blind man tapping.
On dark Edwardian sofas,
   White men napping.

In half-caste twilight, heartfelt
   Songs to Jesus.
Across the arid land,
   Ocean breezes.
The sibilance of sadness
   Never ceases.

The empty cistern.
   The broken Victrola.
The rusted praise of
   Coca-Cola.

Old yellow tablecloths,
   And tea, and hairy
Goats, and airmail
   Stationery.

Copies of *Punch* and *Ebony*.
   Few flowers.
Just the many-petalled sun above
   The endless hours.

FEBRUARY 22

Three boys, American, in dungarees,
walk at a slant across the street
against the mild slant of the winter sun,
moseying out this small, still holiday.

The back of the cold is broken; later snows
will follow, mixed with rain, but today
the macadam is bare, the sun loops high,
and the trees are bathed in sweet grayness.

He was a perfect hero: a man of stone,
as colorless as a monument,
anonymous as Shakespeare. We know him
only as the author of his deeds.

There may have been a man: a surveyor,
a wencher, a temper, a stubborn farmer's mind;
but our legends seem impertinent
graffiti scratched upon his polished granite.

He gazes at us from our dollar bills
reproachfully, a strange green lady,
heavy-lidded, niggle-lipped, and wigged,
who served us better than we have deserved.

More than great successes, we love great failures.
Lincoln is Messiah; he, merely Caesar.
He suffered greatness like a curse.
He fathered our country, we feel, without great joy.

But let us love him now, for he crossed the famous ice,
brought us out of winter, stood, and surveyed
the breadth of our land exulting in the sun:
looked forward to the summer that is past.

VERMONT

Here green is king again,
Usurping honest men.
Like Brazilian cathedrals gone under to creepers,
Gray silos mourn their keepers.

Here ski tows
And shy cows
Alone pin the ragged slopes to the earth
Of profitable worth.

Hawks, professors,
And summering ministers
Roost on the mountainsides of poverty
And sniff the poetry,

And every year
The big black bear,
Slavering through the woods with scrolling mouth,
Comes further south.

FEVER

I have brought back a good message from the land of 102°:
God exists.
I had seriously doubted it before;
but the bedposts spoke of it with utmost confidence,
the threads in my blanket took it for granted,
the tree outside the window dismissed all complaints,
and I have not slept so justly for years.
It is hard, now, to convey
how emblematically appearances sat
upon the membranes of my consciousness;
but it is a truth long known,
that some secrets are hidden from health.

EARTHWORM

We pattern our Heaven
on bright butterflies,
but it must be that even
in earth Heaven lies.

The worm we uproot
in turning a spade
returns, careful brute,
to the peace he has made.

God blesses him; he
gives praise with his toil,
lends comfort to me,
and aerates the soil.

Immersed in the facts,
one must worship there;
claustrophobia attacks
us even in air.

BOIL

In the night the white skin
cries aloud to be broken,
but finds itself a cruel prison;
so it is with reason,
which holds the terror in,
undoubted though the infection.

MY CHILDREN AT THE DUMP

The day before divorce, I take my children
on this excursion;
they are enchanted by
a wonderland of discard where
each complicated star cries out
to be a momentary toy.

To me, too, the waste seems wonderful.
Sheer hills of television tubes, pale lakes
of excelsior, landslides
of perfectly carved carpentry-scraps,
sparkplugs like nuggets, cans iridescent
as peacock plumes, an entire lawnmower
all pluck at my instinct to conserve.

I cannot. These things
were considered, and dismissed
for a reason. But my children
wander wondering among tummocks of junk
like stunted starvelings cruelly set free
at a heaped banquet of food too rich to eat.
I shout, "Don't touch the broken glass!"

The distant metal delicately rusts.
The net effect is floral: a seaward wind
makes flags of cellophane and upright weeds.
The seagulls weep; my boys bring back
bent tractors, hoping what some other child
once played to death can be revived by them.

No. I say, "No." I came to add
my fragments to this universe of loss,
purging my house, ridding a life
no longer shared of remnants.
My daughter brings a naked armless doll,
still hopeful in its dirty weathered eyes,
and I can only tell her, "Love it now.
Love it now, but we can't take it home."

THE GREAT SCARF OF BIRDS

Playing golf on Cape Ann in October,
I saw something to remember.

Ripe apples were caught like red fish in the nets
of their branches. The maples
were colored like apples,
part orange and red, part green.
The elms, already transparent trees,
seemed swaying vases full of sky. The sky
was dramatic with great straggling V's
of geese streaming south, mare's-tails above them;
their trumpeting made us look up and around.
The course sloped into salt marshes,
and this seemed to cause the abundance of birds.

As if out of the Bible
or science fiction,
a cloud appeared, a cloud of dots
like iron filings which a magnet
underneath the paper undulates.
It dartingly darkened in spots,
paled, pulsed, compressed, distended, yet
held an identity firm: a flock
of starlings, as much one thing as a rock.
One will moved above the trees
the liquid and hesitant drift.

Come nearer, it became less marvellous,
more legible, and merely huge.
"I never saw so many birds!" my partner claimed;
we returned our eyes to the game.
Later, as Lot's wife must have done,
in a pause of walking, not thinking
of calling down a consequence,
I shifted my bag and looked back.

*

The rise of the fairway behind us was tinted,
so evenly tinted I might not have noticed
but that at the rim of the delicate shadow
the starlings were thicker and outlined the flock
as an inkstain in drying pronounces its edges.
The gradual rise of green was vastly covered;
I had thought nothing in nature could be so broad but grass.

And as
I watched, one bird,
prompted by accident or will to lead,
ceased resting; and, lifting in a casual billow,
the flock ascended as a lady's scarf,
transparent, of gray, might be twitched
by one corner, drawn upward, and then,
decided against, negligently tossed toward a chair:
dissolving all anxiety,
the southward cloud withdrew into the air.

Long had it been since my heart
had been lifted as it was by the lifting of that great scarf.

HOEING

I sometimes fear the younger generation will be deprived
  of the pleasures of hoeing;
  there is no knowing
how many souls have been formed by this simple exercise.

The dry earth like a great scab breaks, revealing
  moist-dark loam—
  the pea-root's home,
a fertile wound perpetually healing.

How neatly the green weeds go under!
  The blade chops the earth new.
  Ignorant the wise boy who
has never rendered thus the world fecunder.

FIREWORKS

These spasms and chrysanthemums of light
are like emotions
exploding under a curved night that corresponds
to the dark firmament within.

See, now, the libidinous flare,
spinning on its stick in vain resistance
to the upright ego and mortality's gravity;
behold, above, the sudden bloom,
turquoise, each tip a comet,
of pride—followed, after an empty bang,
by an ebbing amber galaxy, despair.

We feel our secrets bodied forth like flags
as wide as half the sky. Now
passions, polychrome and coruscating, crowd
one upon the other in a final fit,
a terminal display
that tilts the children's faces back in bleached dismay
and sparks an infant's crying in the grass.

They do not understand, the younger ones,
what thunderheads and nebulae,
what waterfalls and momentary roses fill
the world's one aging skull,
and are relieved when in a falling veil
the last awed outburst crumbles to reveal
the pattern on the playroom wall
of tame and stable stars.

FROM POSTCARDS FROM SOVIET CITIES

Moscow

Gold onions rooted in the sky
Grow downward into sullen, damp
Museums where, with leaden eye,
Siberian tourists dumbly tramp.

The streets are wide as silences.
The cobblestones between the GUM
And Kremlin echo—an abyss
Lies sealed within a giant room.

The marble box where Lenin sleeps
Receives the Tartar gaze of those
Who come from where Far Russia keeps
Her counsels wrapped in deadening snows.

St. Basil's, near at hand, erects
The swirlings that so charmed the czar
He blinded both the architects
To keep such beauty singular.

Leningrad

"To build a window on the west"
Great Peter came to Neva's mouth
And found a swamp, which he oppressed
With stones imported from the south.

The city, subtly polychrome
(Old ochre, green, and dull maroon),
Can make Italians feel at home
Beneath the tilted arctic noon.

The Palace holds, pistachio,
A wilderness of treasure where
The ghosts of plump czarinas go
On dragging diamonds up the stair.

Suburban acres of the dead
Memorialize the Siege, a hell
Of blackened snow and watered bread.
Some couples Twist in our hotel.

Kiev

Clutching his cross, St. Vladimir
Gazes with eyes that seem to grieve
Across the sandy Dnieper, where
He baptized godforsaken Kiev.

Now deconverted trolleys turn
Around the square, emitting sparks.
The churches, cold as attics, burn
With gilt above the poplar parks.

Beneath the earth, in catacombs,
Dried patriarchs lie mummified;
Brocaded silk enmeshed with bones
Offends our trim, mascaraed guide,

Who, driving homeward, gestures toward
The ruins of Moussorgsky's Gate—
Like some old altar, unrestored,
Where peasant women supplicate.

Yerevan

Armenia, Asia's waif, has here
At last constructed shelter proof
Against all Turkish massacre.
A soft volcanic rock called tuff

Carves easily and serves to be
The basis of the boulevards
That lead from slums of history
Into a future stripped of swords.

The crescent-shaped hotel is rose
And looks toward Lenin Square and tan
Dry mountains down which power flows
From turbines lodged in Lake Sevan.

Mount Ararat, a conscience, floats
Cloudlike, in sight but unpossessed,
For there, where Noah docked his boat,
Begins the brutal, ancient West.

ROMAN PORTRAIT BUSTS

Others in museums pass them by,
but I, I
am drawn like a maggot to meat
by their pupilless eyes
and their putrefying individuality.

They are, these Livias and Marcuses,
these pouting dead Octavias,
no two alike: never has art
so whorishly submitted
to the importunities of the real.

In good conscience one must admire
the drab lack of exaggeration,
the way each head,
crone's, consul's, or child's,
is neither bigger nor smaller than life.

Their eyes taste awful.
It is vile,
deliciously, to see selves so
unsoftened by history, such
indigestible gristle.

DOG'S DEATH

She must have been kicked unseen or brushed by a car.
Too young to know much, she was beginning to learn
To use the newspapers spread on the kitchen floor
And to win, wetting there, the words, "Good dog! Good dog!"

We thought her shy malaise was a shot reaction.
The autopsy disclosed a rupture in her liver.
As we teased her with play, blood was filling her skin
And her heart was learning to lie down forever.

Monday morning, as the children were noisily fed
And sent to school, she crawled beneath the youngest's bed.
We found her twisted and limp but still alive.
In the car to the vet's, on my lap, she tried

To bite my hand and died. I stroked her warm fur
And my wife called in a voice imperious with tears.
Though surrounded by love that would have upheld her,
Nevertheless she sank and, stiffening, disappeared.

Back home, we found that in the night her frame,
Drawing near to dissolution, had endured the shame
Of diarrhoea and had dragged across the floor
To a newspaper carelessly left there. *Good dog.*

MEMORIES OF ANGUILLA, 1960

The boy who came at night
to light the Tilley lamps
(they hissed, too bright;
he always looked frightened)
in the morning dragged his bait pail
through the beryl seawater
sauntering barelegged
without once looking down.

The night Rebecca's—
she lived beneath us—
sailor lover returned from sea
and beat her for hours,
it was as hard to sleep as the time
she tied a rooster
inside an oil drum.

The woman across the road,
pregnant by an annual visit,
cursed ungratefully, tossing rocks
at her weeping children.
The radio on her windowsill
played hymns from Antigua all day.

And the black children in blue
trotted down the white-dust road
to learn cricket and Victorian history,
and the princesses
balancing water drawn
from the faucet by our porch
held their heads at an insolent angle.

The constellations
that evaded our naming.
The blind man. The drunk.

The albino,
his fat lips blistered by the sun.
The beaches empty of any hotel.
Dear island of such poor beauty,
meekly waiting to rebel.

TOPSFIELD FAIR

Animals seem so sad to be themselves—
the turkey a turkey even to his wattle,
the rabbit with his pink, distinctly, eyes,
the prize steer humble in his stall.
What are they thinking, the pouter pigeons,
shaped like opulent ladies' hats,
jerking and staring in aisles of cages;
what does the mute meek monkey say?

Our hearts go out to them, then stop:
our fellows in mortality, like us
stiff-thrust into marvellous machines
tight-packed with chemical commands
to breathe, blink, feed, sniff, mate,
and, stuck like stamps in species, go out of date.

DREAM OBJECTS

Strangest is their reality,
their three-dimensional workmanship:
veined pebbles that have an underside,
maps one could have studied for minutes longer,
books we seem to read page after page.

If these are symbols cheaply coined
to buy the mind a momentary pardon,
whence this extravagance? Fine
as dandelion polls, they surface and explode
in the wind of the speed of our dreaming,

so that we awake with the sense
of having missed everything, tourists
hustled by bus through a land whose history
is our rich history, whose artifacts
were filed to perfection by beggars we fear.

MIDPOINT

I. Introduction

ARGUMENT: The poet begins, and describes his beginnings. Early intimations of wonder and dread. His family on the Hill of Life in 1939, and his own present uncomfortable maturity. Refusing to take good advice, he insists on the endurance of the irreducible.

Of nothing but me, me
—all wrong, all wrong—
as I cringe in the face of glory

I sing, lacking another song.
Proud mouths around me clack
that the livelong day is long

but the nip of night tugs back
my would-be celebrant brain
to the bricks of the moss-touched walk,

the sweet cold grass that had no name,
the arbor, and the wicker chair
turned cavernous beneath the tapping rain.

Plain wood and paint pressed back my stare.
Stiff cardboard apples crayoned to sell
(for nickels minted out of air)

from orange crates with still a citrus smell:
the thermometer: the broom:
this code of things contrived to tell

a timid God of a continuum
wherein he was delimited.
Vengeful, he applied his sense of doom

with tricycle tires to coppery-red
anthills and, dizzy in his Heaven, grieved
above his crushed Inferno of the dead.

A screen of color said, *You are alive.*
A skin of horror floated at my feet.
The corpses, comma-shaped, indicted, *If*

a wheel from far above (in summer heat,
loose thunders roamed the sky like untongued wagons)
would turn, you'd lie squashed on the street.

That bright side porch in Shillington:
under the sun, beneath grape leaves,
I feared myself an epiphenomenon.

The crucial question was, *Why am I me?*
In China boys were born as cherishing
of their small selves; in buried Greece

their swallowed spirits wink
like mica lost in marble.
Sickened by Space's waste, I tried to cling

to the thought of the indissoluble:
a point infinitely hard
was luminous in me, and cried *I will.*

I sought in middling textures part-
icles of iridescence, scintillae
in dullish surfaces; and pictured art

as my descending, via pencil, into dry
exactitude. Behind the beaded curtain
of Matter lurked an understanding Eye.

Clint Shilling's drawing lessons: in
the sun he posed an egg on paper, and said
a rainbow ran along the shadow's rim—

the rainbow at the edge of the shadow of the egg.
My kindergarten eyes were sorely strained
to see it there. My still-soft head

began to ache, but docilely I feigned
the purple ghosts of green in clumsy wax:
thus was I early trained

and wonder, now, if Clint were orthodox.
He lived above a spikestone-studded wall
and honed his mustache like a tiny ax

and walked a brace of collies down our alley
in Pennsylvania dusk
beside his melodic wife, white-haired and tall.

O Philadelphia Avenue! My eyes lift up
from the furtive pencilled paper
and drown, are glad to drown, in a flood

of light, of trees and houses: our neighbors
live higher than we, in gaunt
two-family houses glaring toward our arbor.

Five-fingered leaves hold horse chestnuts.
The gutter runs with golden water
from Flickinger's ice plant. Telephone wires hunt

through the tree crowns under orders
to find the wider world
the daily *Eagle* and the passing autos

keep hinting the existence of. And girls
stroll toward Lancaster Avenue and school
in the smoke of burning leaves, in the swirl

of snow, in the cruel
brilliance that follows, in the storm of buds that marries
earth to the iron sky and brings renewal

to the town so wide and fair from quarry
to trolley tracks, from Kenhorst to Mohnton,
from farmers' market to cemetery,

that a boy might feel himself point N
in optics, where plane ABCD—
a visual phenomenon—

converges and passes through to be
(inverted on the other side,
where film or retina receives it)

a kind of afterlife,
knife-lifted out of flux
and developed out of time:

the night sky, with a little luck,
was a camera back, the constellations
faint silver salts, and I the crux

of radii, the tip of two huge cones,
called Empyrean and Earth,
that took their slant and spin from me alone.

I was that N, that white-hot nothing, yet
my hands, my penis, came also into view,
and as I grew I half unwilling learned

to seem a creature, to subdue
my giant solipsism to a common scale.
Reader, it is pure bliss to share with you

the plight of love, the fate
of death, the need for food,
the privileges of ignorance, the ways

of traffic, competition, and remorse.
I look upon my wife, and marvel that
a woman, competent and good,

has shared these years; my children, protein-fat,
echo my eyes and my laugh: I am disarmed
to think that my body has mattered,

has been enrolled like a red-faced farm-
boy in the beautiful country club
of mankind's copulating swarm.

I did not expect it; humble
as a glow-worm, my boneless ego asked
only to witness, to serve as the hub

of a wheeling spectacle that would not pass.
My parents, my impression was,
had acted out all parts on my behalf;

their shouting and their silences
in the hissing bedroom dark
scorched the shadows; a ring of ashes

expanded with each smoldering remark
and left no underbrush of fuel
of passion for my intimidated spark.

My mother's father squeezed his Bible
sighing, and smoked five-cent cigars
behind the chickenhouse, exiling the smell.

His wife, bespectacled Granma,
beheaded the chickens
in their gritty wire yard

and had a style of choking during dinner;
she'd run to the porch, where one of us
would pound her on the back until her inner

conflict had resolved. Like me, she was nervous;
I had sympathetic stomach cramps.
We were, perhaps, too close,

the five of us. Our lamps
were dim, our carpets worn, the furniture
hodgepodge and venerable and damp.

And yet I never felt that we were poor.
Our property included several stray
cats, one walnut tree, a hundred feet or more

of privet hedge, and fresh ice every other day.
The brothers pressing to be born
were kept, despite their screams, offstage.

The fifth point of a star, I warmed
to my onliness, threw tantrums,
and, for my elders' benison, performed.

Seven I was when to amuse them
I drew the Hill of Life.
My grandfather, a lusty sixty-some,

is near the bottom, beside
the Tree to God, though twice twelve years
in fact would pass before he, ninety, died,

of eating an unwashed peach.
His wife, crippled but chipper, stepped
above him downward and, true, did not precede

him up that Tree, but snored and slept
six seasons more before her speechless spirit
into unresisted silence crept.

A gap, and then my father, Mr.
Downdike of high-school hilarity,
strides manful down the dry, unslippery

pencil line. My mother is at the peak—
eleven days short of thirty-five—
and starting up the lonely slope is me,

dear Chonny. Now on the downward side
behold me: my breath is short,
though my parents are still alive.

For conscientious climbing, God gave me these rewards:
fame with its bucket of unanswerable letters,
wealth with its worrisome market report,

rancid advice from my critical betters,
a drafty house, a voluptuous spouse,
and *quatre enfants*—none of them bed-wetters.

From *Time*'s grim cover, my fretful face peers out.
Ten thousand soggy mornings have warped my lids
and minced a crafty pulp of this my mouth;

and yet, incapable of being dimmed,
there harbors still inside me like the light
an anchored ketch displays, among my ribs,

a hopeful burning riding out the tide
that this strange universe employs
to strip itself of wreckage in the night.

"Take stock. Repent. The motion that destroys
creates elsewhere; the looping sun
sees no world twice." False truths! I vouch for boys

impatient, inartistically, to get things done,
armored in speckled cardboard
and an untoward faith in the eye/I pun.

II. The Photographs

ARGUMENT: The pictures speak for themselves. A cycle of growth, mating, and birth. The coarse dots, calligraphic and abstract, become faces, with troubled expressions. Distance improves vision. Lost time sifts through these immutable old screens.

III. The Dance of the Solids

ARGUMENT: In stanzas associated with allegory the actual atomic structure of solids unfolds. Metals, Ceramics, and Polymers. The conduction of heat, electricity, and light; nonsymmetry and magnetism. Solidity emerges as intricate and giddy.

All things are Atoms: Earth and Water, Air
 And Fire, all, *Democritus* foretold.
 Swiss *Paracelsus*, in's alchemic lair,
 Saw Sulphur, Salt, and Mercury unfold
 Amid Millennial hopes of faking Gold.
 Lavoisier dethroned Phlogiston; then
 Molecular Analysis made bold
 Forays into the gases: Hydrogen
Stood naked in the dazzled sight of Learned Men.

The Solid State, however, kept its grains
 Of Microstructure coarsely veiled until
 X-ray diffraction pierced the Crystal Planes
 That roofed the giddy Dance, the taut Quadrille
 Where Silicon and Carbon Atoms will
 Link Valencies, four-figured, hand in hand
 With common Ions and Rare Earths to fill
 The lattices of Matter, Salt or Sand,
With tiny Excitations, quantitively grand.

The *Metals*, lustrous Monarchs of the Cave,
 Are ductile and conductive and opaque
 Because each Atom generously gave
 Its own Electrons to a mutual Stake,
 A Pool that acts as Bond. The Ions take
 The stacking shape of Spheres, and slip and flow
 When pressed or dented; thusly *Metals* make
 A better Paper Clip than a Window,
Are vulnerable to Shear, and, heated, brightly glow.

Ceramic, muddy Queen of Human Arts,
First served as simple Stone. Feldspar supplied
Crude Clay; and Rubies, Porcelain, and Quartz
Came each to light. Aluminum Oxide
Is typical—a *Metal* close-allied
With Oxygen ionically; no free
Electrons form a lubricating tide,
Hence, Empresslike, *Ceramics* tend to be
Resistant, porous, brittle, and refractory.

Prince *Glass*, *Ceramic*'s son, though crystal-clear,
Is no wise crystalline. The fond Voyeur
And Narcissist alike devoutly peer
Into Disorder, the Disorderer
Being Covalent Bondings that prefer
Prolonged Viscosity and spread loose nets
Photons slip through. The average *Polymer*
Enjoys a Glassy state, but cools, forgets
To slump, and clouds in closely patterned Minuets.

The *Polymers*, those giant Molecules,
Like Starch and Polyoxymethylene,
Flesh out, as protein Serfs and plastic Fools,
This Kingdom with Life's Stuff. Our time has seen
The synthesis of Polyisoprene
And many cross-linked Helixes unknown
To *Robert Hooke*, but each primordial Bean
Knew Cellulose by heart. *Nature* alone
Of Collagen and Apatite compounded Bone.

What happens in these Lattices when *Heat*
Transports Vibrations through a solid mass?
$T = 3Nk$ is much too neat;
A rigid Crystal's not a fluid Gas.
Debye in 1912 proposed Elas-

Tic Waves called *phonons* that obey *Max Planck's*
$E = h\nu$. Though amorphous *Glass*,
Umklapp Switchbacks, and Isotopes play Pranks
Upon his Formulae, *Debye* deserves warm Thanks.

Electroconductivity depends
On Free Electrons: in Germanium
A touch of Arsenic liberates; in blends
Like Nickel Oxide, *Ohms* thwart Current. From
Pure Copper threads to wads of Chewing Gum
Resistance varies hugely. Cold and Light
As well as "doping" modify the sum
Of *Fermi* levels, Ion scatter, site
Proximity, and other Factors recondite.

Textbooks and Heaven only are Ideal;
Solidity is an imperfect state.
Within the cracked and dislocated Real
Nonstoichiometric Crystals dominate.
Stray Atoms sully and precipitate;
Strange holes, *excitons*, wander loose; because
Of Dangling Bonds, a chemical Substrate
Corrodes and catalyzes—surface Flaws
Help Epitaxial Growth to fix adsorptive claws.

White Sunlight, *Newton* saw, is not so pure;
A Spectrum bared the Rainbow to his view.
Each Element absorbs its signature:
Go add a negative Electron to
Potassium Chloride; it turns deep blue,
As Chromium incarnadines Sapphire.
Wavelengths, absorbed, are reëmitted through
Fluorescence, Phosphorescence, and the higher
Intensities that deadly *Laser Beams* require.

Magnetic Atoms, such as Iron, keep
   Unpaired Electrons in their middle shell,
   Each one a spinning Magnet that would leap
   The *Bloch Walls* whereat antiparallel
   Domains converge. Diffuse Material
   Becomes *Magnetic* when another Field
   Aligns domains, like Seaweed in a swell.
   How nicely Microscopic Forces yield,
In Units growing visible, the World we wield!

IV. The Play of Memory

ARGUMENT: The poet remembers and addresses those he has loved. Certain equations emerge from the welter, in which Walt Whitman swims. Arrows urge us on. Imagery from Canto II returns, enlarged. Sonnet to his father. Conception as climax of pointillism theme.

At the foot of the playground slide

FEET, →

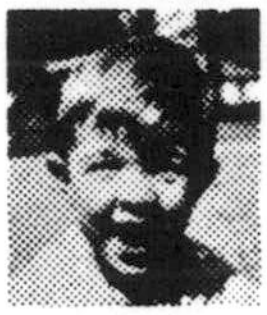

striking the dust,
had worn a trough
that after a rain
became a puddle.

Last night

lying listening to rain

myriads of points of sound

myriads

memory of girl—worker for McCarthy—came to our door—zaftig—lent her my wife's bathing suit—she pinned it—she was smaller than my wife—pinned it to fit—the house upstairs hushed—velvety sense of summer dust—she came down—we went to beach—talked politics lying on pebbles—her skin so pale—bra too big so the curve of her breast was revealed nearly to the nipple—"If he ever got any real power it'd ruin him for me"—pebbles hurt her young skin—we came home—she took shower—should have offered to wash her back—passing me on the way to the bathroom—skin—dawn-colored skin—eyes avoided—eye/I—I should have offered to wash her back—dressed in her own cool clothes, she handed me back the bathing suit, unpinned again—lovely skin of her arms untanned from a summer of campaigning by telephone—strange cool nerve taking a shower in married man's wifeless home—the velvety summer dust waiting to be stirred, to be loved, by the fan—left her by South Green—"You'll be all right"—"Oh sure"—girls hitchhike now—a silk-skinned harem drifting through this conscience-stricken nation

CLEAN GENE

and empty arms

I made a note for this poem

in the dark

Where am I?

ALL

wrong, all wrong

myriads

window mullions

dust motes

Sense of Many Things

what was being said through them?

S o m e t h i n g

"huh?"

also we
used to
play hop-
scotch
with a
rubber heel ⟶ **1**

2

3

4 5

6 7

8

9 10 *"Hey!"*

↓

You who used to swing on the pavilion rafters
showing me your underpants
you with whom I came six times in one night
back from St. Thomas sunburned
in my haste to return

my skin peeling from my chest like steamed wallpaper
my prick toward morning a battered miracle
of response
and your good mouth wetter than any warm washrag
and the walk afterwards toward the Park
past Doubleday's packed with my books
your fucked-out insides airy in your smile
and my manner a proud boy's
after some stunt
did you know you were showing me your underpants?
did you know they said you laid
beneath the pines by the poorhouse dam?
and in the Algonquin you
in the persimmon nightie just down to your pussy
and your air of distraction
your profile harassed against the anonymous wall
that sudden stooping kiss
a butterfly on my glans
your head beat like a wing on the pillow
your whimper in the car
you wiped blood from me with a Kleenex
by the big abandoned barn I never drive past
without suffering
you who outran me at fox-in-the-morning
whom I caught on the steps of the Fogg
the late games of Botticelli
you in your bed Ann in hers
and the way we would walk to the window
overlooking the bird sanctuary
our hands cool on each other's genitals
have you forgotten?
we always exuded better sex than we had
should I have offered to wash your back?
you whose breast I soaped
and you my cock, and your cunt
indivisible from the lather and huge as a purse and the mirror
giving us back ourselves

I said look because we were so beautiful and
you said "we're very ordinary"
and in the Caribbean the night you knelt
to be taken from behind and we were entangled
with the mosquito netting
and in the woods you let me hold your breasts
your lipstick all flecked
the twigs dissolved in the sky above and I jerked off
driving home alone one-handed
singing of you
you
who demurely clenched
your thighs and came and might have snapped my neck
you who nursed me
and fed me dreams of Manhattan in the cloudy living room
and rubbed my sore chest with VapoRub
and betrayed me with my father
and laughed it off
and betrayed me with your husband
and laughed it off
and betrayed me beneath the pines
and never knew I thought I knew
your underpants were ghostly gray and now
you wear them beneath your nightie
and shy from my hug
pubescent
my daughter
who when I twirled you and would not stop bit my leg
on West Thirteenth Street
you who lowered your bathing suit in the dunes
your profile distracted against the sand
your hips a table
holding a single treat
your breasts hors d'oeuvres
you fed me tomatoes until I vomited
because you wanted me to grow and you
said my writing was "a waste" about "terrible people"
and tried to call me down from the tree

for fear I'd fall
and sat outside nodding while I did toidy
because I was afraid of ghosts
and said to me "the great thing about us is
you're sure of the things I'm unsure about and
I'm sure of the things you're unsure about"
and you blamed yourself for my colds
and my skin and my gnawing panic to excel, you
walked with me on Penn Street
the day I tried to sell cartoons to Pomeroy's
and they took our picture **LOANS**
Oh Mother above
our heads it said
LOANS

I think of you and mirrors:
the one that hung in the front hall
murky and flyspecked and sideways
and the little round one with which you
conducted arcane examinations by the bedside
I lying on the bed and not daring
look over the edge
I was a child and as an infant
I had cracked this mirror in a tantrum
it had a crack
it was a crack
O
→ **MIRRORS ARE VAGINAS**
and everywhere I go I plunge my gaze
into this lustrous openness
to see if I have grown

“Prodigal, you have given me love!
Therefore I to you give love!”
“O I am wonderful!
I cannot tell how my ankles bend”
“The smallest sprout shows
there is really no death”
“And the pismire is equally perfect,
and a grain of sand,
and the egg of the wren”
“What is commonest, cheapest,
nearest, easiest, is Me”

Given **M** = **V**
and sex as a “knowing”;
“knowing” = “seeing”

∴ **PENISES ARE EYES**

“his eyes shut and a bird flying below us he was shy all the same I liked him like that moaning I made him blush a little when I got over him that way when I unbuttoned him and took his out and drew back the skin it had a kind of eye in it”

Q.E.D.

and you who sat
and so beautifully listened
your gray hair limpid and tense like a forest pool
“nor whence the cause of my faintest wish”
listened as I too effortlessly talked
after putting on my glasses
(you called them my “magic eyes”)

shielding my genitals (remember
                    the Cocteau movie where he slashes an egg?
not to mention poor Gloucester's
          "vile jelly")
talked but never explicit anent sex
          "shy all the same"
trying to wheedle your love
          and after months and years
you pronounced at last:
          "are demonstrations of flying ability to this ugly earth-

          mother figure, successively incarnated in the husbands,
          rather than true relationships with the women"
"Oh,"

I said, "how sad if true"
     staggering out past the next patient
          in that room of old *Newsweeks*
               cured
sing   *oh*
     "adulterous offers made, acceptances,
               rejections with convex lips"
"Copulation is no more rank
               to me than death is"
"And mossy scabs of the worm fence,
               and heap'd stones, elder,
                    mullen and poke-weed"
and Mother those three-way mirrors
          in Croll & Keck's you
               buying me my year's jacket
my Joseph's coat
          I saw my appalling profile
and the bulge at the back of my head
          as if my brain were pregnant
"apart from the pulling and hauling stands what I am"
     I felt you saw me as a fountain spouting
gray pool unruffled as you listened to me
     telling cleverly how I loved the mail

how on Philadelphia Avenue I would lie
in the hall with the flecked mirror
waiting for Mr. Miller
to plop the mail through the slot
spilling over me
MALE/MAIL
letter-slots are vaginas
and stamps are semen swimming in the dark
engraved with DNA
"vile jelly"
and mailboxes wait capaciously to be fucked
throughout the town as I insomniac
you pet
"To touch my person to some one else's
is about as much as I can stand"
"And I know I am solid and sound"
"The well-taken photographs—
but your wife or friend close and solid in your arms?"

"I tighten her all night to my thighs and lips"
the bed of two beds in the cabin
whose levels did not meet
the pine needles myriad about us
and the double-decker bunk
so that mounting me you bumped your
head
and the sleeping bag spread
on the lawn by the saltwater inlet
ow

mosquitoes
myriads

. . . .

scintillations of grass
conversation of distant water
"The play of shine and shade
on the trees as the supple boughs wag"
What is pressing through?
take me
"For every atom belonging to me,
as good belongs to you"
rien
"And nothing, not God,
is greater to one than one's self is"
à trente et six ans
"Behavior lawless as snow-flakes"
having waited out numerous dead nights with listening
and with prayer
having brought myself back from the dead with extra-
vagant motions of the mind
the slide
the puddle
the clack of box hockey
the pavilion
many years later you
sat on my lap at a class reunion
your fanny was girdled and hard
a mother of four and I the father of four
your body metallic with sex
and I was so happy I stuttered
perhaps Creation is a stutter of the Void
(I could revise the universe if I just knew math)
I think it may all turn out to be an illusion

the red shift merely travel fatigue
and distance losing its value like inflated currency
(physicists are always so comfortably talking
about infinite flashlight beams
and men on frictionless roller skates)
and the atom a wrinkle that imagines itself
and mass a factor of our own feebleness
"And to die is different from what any one supposed,
and luckier"
and if my body is history
then my ego is Christ
and no inversion is too great for me
no fate too special
a drowning man cannot pull
himself out by his own hair (Barth)

"the
ant's a
centaur
in his
dragon
world"

and you above me in the bunk
coming and crying, "Fuck, John!"
all our broken veins displayed
the honey of your coming a hummingbird's tongue
an involuntary coo
you pulled
j'ai pensé que
having inwardly revolved numerous Protestant elements—screen doors, worn Bibles, rubber condoms that snap and hurt, playground grass that feet have beaten into a dusty fuzz, certain Popsicle pleasures and hours of real reading, dental pain, the sociable rasp of Sunday drinks, the roses dozing, the children bored—

where you were always present
whose shampooed groin
held all I wished to know—
(dance, words!)
I deduced
a late bloomer but an early comer
my works both green and overripe
(Proust spurred me to imitation,
the cars a-swish on Riverside Drive,

and Kierkegaard held back the dark waters, but)
je suis arrivé à la pensée que

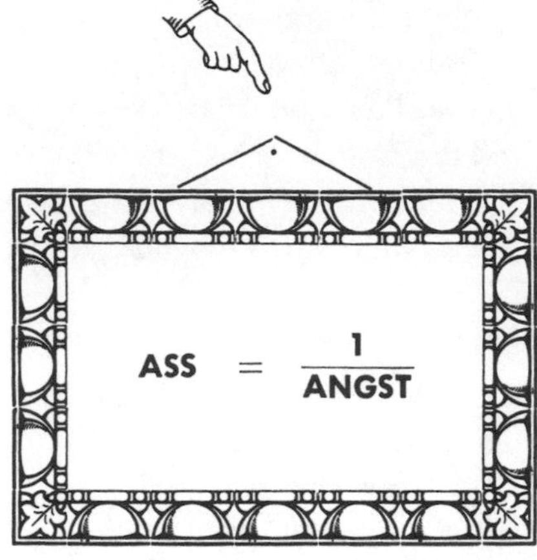

you pulled me up
I did fly
joy pulled a laugh from me
your hands, voice fluttered
"Is that funny? Is it?"
your nerves, voice tumbling
a two-body circus

thank you

the taint of performance

forgive me

your
face

your
tense
hand

your
good
sad
shoes

“In vain the mastodon retreats
beneath its own powder'd bones”
these dreadful nights of dust
of discrete and cretin thoughts
the mind searching for a virtue
whereon to pillow and be oblivious
“The palpable is in its place,
and the impalpable is in its place”
rummaging amid old ecstasies
“your poetry began to go to pot
when you took up fucking housewives”
a hitching post for the heart
the devil rides in circles

1 2 3 4 6 7 9 8 01

all wrong

wherever we turn we find a curved steel wall
of previous speculation
and the water leaking from the main conduits
and the gauges rising
the needles shivering like whipped bitches
“The nearest gnat is an explanation,
and a drop or motion of waves a key”
“I effuse my flesh in eddies,
and drift in lacy jags”

try again

FATHER, as old as you when I was four,
I feel the restlessness of nearing death
But lack your manic passion to endure,
Your Stoic fortitude and Christian faith.

Remember, at the blackboard, factoring?
My life at midpoint seems a string of terms
In which an error clamps the hidden spring
Of resolution cancelling confirms.
Topheavy Dutchmen sundered from the sea,
Bewitched by money, believing in riddles
Syrian vagrants propagated, we
Incline to live by what the world belittles.
  God screws the lukewarm, slays the heart that faints,
  And saves His deepest silence for His saints.

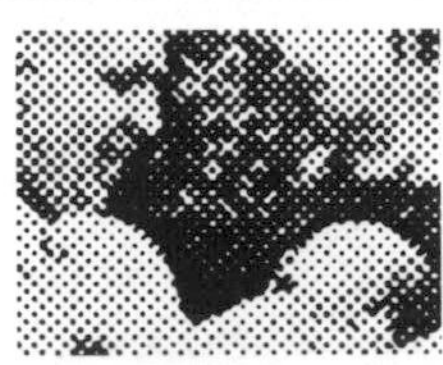

I am a paper bag
      I am trying to punch my way out of
"Out of the dimness opposite equals advance—
      always substance and increase,
            always sex"

let's go

"Always a knit of identity—
      always distinction—
            always a breed of life"
you who breathe beside me
      on Sparks Street spilled your cool nudity
across my eyes
            above the summer dust
   body of ivory I have marred, silk I have stretched
you came against me kneeling
      while a truck passed rumbling below

and in Vermont
the only souls in a square mile of mountain
the mantle lamps
the deck of cards
the Unitarian paperbacks
the spinning wheel gnawed by a porcupine
we, too, had our violence
"The butcher-boy puts off his killing clothes"
beside me like a sacrifice
mildly curious as to the knife
we did conceive
in that square mile of wooded loneliness
a twinned point began to ravel
you took me in
"the fish-eggs are in their place"
most gracious

"The
garden
is a
river
flowing
south"

merci

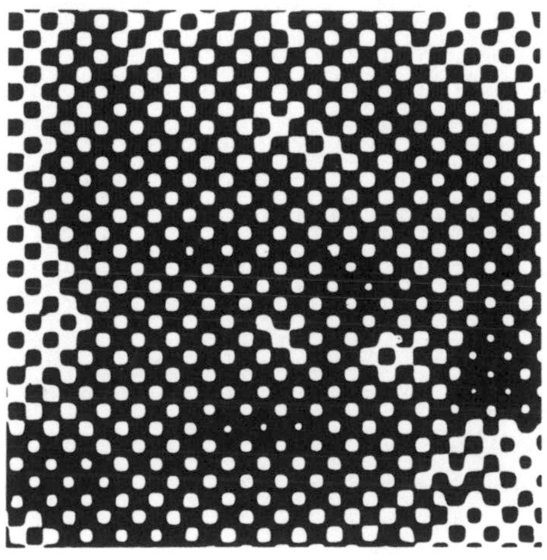

V. Conclusion

ARGUMENT: The poet strives to conclude, but his aesthetic of dots prevents him. His heroes are catalogued. World politics: a long view. Intelligent hedonistic advice. Chilmark Pond in August. He appears to accept, reluctantly, the advice.

An easy Humanism plagues the land;
I choose to take an otherworldly stand.
The Archimedean point, however small,
Will serve to lift the whole terrestrial Ball.
Reality transcends itself within;
Atomically all pundits must begin.
The Truth arrives as if by telegraph:
One dot; two dots; a silence; then a laugh.
The rules inhere, and will not be imposed
Ab alto, as most Liberals have supposed.
Praise *Kierkegaard*, who splintered *Hegel*'s creed
Upon the rock of Existential need;
Praise *Barth*, who told how saving Faith can flow
From Terror's oscillating Yes and No;
Praise *Henry Green*, who showed how lifetimes sift
Through gestures, glances, silly talk, and drift.
Praise *Disney*, for dissolving *Goofy*'s stride
Into successive stills our eyes elide,
And *Jan Vermeer*, for salting humble bread
With dabs of light, as well as bricks and thread.
Praise IBM, which boiled the brain's rich stores
Down to a few electric either/ors;
Praise Pointillism, Calculus, and all
That turn the world infinitesimal:
The midget of the alphabet is I;
The Infinite is littleness heaped high.
All wrong, all wrong—throughout phenomena
There gleams the sword of Universal Law;
Elegant formulations sever Chance
From Cause, and clumsy Matter learns to dance.

A magnet subdivides into Domains
Till ratios are reached where Stasis reigns.
An insect's structure limits it: an Ant
Can never swell to be an Elephant.
The Demiurge expands up to a rim
Where calculable cold collapses Him.
  In human matters, too, Inductions act,
Cleave circumstance, and bare the general Fact.
Karl Marx and *Sigmund Freud* together show
Oppression alternates with Overthrow.
The proletarian Id combines its mass
With Superego's castellated class
To pinch the bourgeois Ego out of power.
The flag of Anarchy besports a flower;
The telescopic cock and winking cunt
Emblazon Urban Youth's united front.
  The world boils over; Ho and Mao and Che
Blood-red inaugurate a brighter day.
Apocalypse is in; mad Eros drives
The continents upon a shoal of lives.
Awash with wealth, the fair Republic creaks,
While boilermen below enlarge the leaks;
What child is this, who gathers up still more
Confetti from the tilting ballroom floor?

  Well, times are always desperate; our strange
Earth greets the old catastrophe of Change.
In bins of textbooks, holocausts lie stacked:
"No life was spared when Genghis Khan attacked."
It little counts in History's jaded eye
Just how we copulate, or how we die.
Six million Jews will join the Congolese
King Leopold of Belgium cleared like trees.
And Hiroshima's epoch-making flash
Will fade as did the hosts of *Gilgamesh.*
The Judgment Day seems nigh to every age;

But History yawns, and turns another page.
Our lovely green-clad mother spreads her legs—
Corrosive, hairy, rank—and, shameless, begs
For Pestilence to fuck her if he can,
For War to come, and come again, again.
The meanwhile, let us live as islanders
Who pluck what fruit the lowered branch proffers.
Each passing moment masks a tender face;
Nothing has had to be, but is by Grace.
Attend to every sunset; greet the dawn
That combs with spears of shade the glistening lawn.
Enjoy the risen morning, upright noon,
Declining day, and swollen leprous moon.
Observe the trees, those clouds of breathing leaf;
Their mass transcends the insect's strident grief.
The forest holds a thousand deaths, yet lives;
The lawn accepts its coat of bone and gives
Next spring a sweeter, graver tone of green.
Gladly the maple seed spins down, between
Two roots extends a tendril, grips beneath
The soil, and suffers the mower's spinning teeth.
Nothing is poorly made; nothing is dull:
The Crabgrass thinks itself adorable.
Cherish your work; take profit in the task:
Doing's the one reward a Man dare ask.
The Wood confides its secrets to the plane;
The Dovetail fits, and reconfirms the Grain.
The white-hot writhing Steel is tonged and plunged,
A-sizzle, into Form, all flecks expunged.
The Linotyper leans above his keys,
And feathers down a ton of journalese;
Engraver and Apprentice, in their room
Of acid baths and photophobic gloom,
Transform to metal dots ten shades of gray,
And herald Everyman's beginning day.
The Clergyman, beside the sighing bed,
Strains for a sign of Credence from the dead.

The Lawyer eagle-eyed for Falsehood's glint,
The Doctor bent on Hardening's murmured hint,
The Biochemist analyzing sera,
The Astrophysicist alone with Lyra,
The Archaeologist with pick and brush,
The Nature-walker having heard a thrush—
Attentiveness! The pinpoint is the locus
Of Excellence in lands of softened focus.
   Applaud your Neighbor; admire his style
That grates upon you like a bastard file.
His trespasses resemble yours in kind;
He, too, is being crowded from behind.
Don't kill; or, if you must, while killing, grieve.
Doubt not; that is, until you can't believe.
Don't covet Mrs. X; or if you do,
Make sure, before you leap, she covets you.
   Like meat upon the table, we will spoil:
Time is the troubled water; Faith, the oil.
The curse of Tempo regulates the dance;
To move necessitates Impermanence.
So flow, flow outward; *Heraclitus* saw,
In Nature's crystalline, the fluid flaw:
Our Guilt inheres in sheer Existing, so
Forgive yourself your death, and freely flow.
   Transcendent Goodness makes elastic claims;
The merciful Creator hid His Aims.
Beware false Gods: the Infallible Man,
The flawless formula, the Five-Year Plan.
Abjure bandwagons; be shy of machines,
Charisma, Ends that justify the Means,
And oaths that bind the postulant to kill
His own Self-love and independent Will.
A Mussolini leads to Hitler; hate
Apostles of the all-inclusive State.
   Half-measures are most human; Compromise,
Inglorious and gray, placates the Wise.
By messianic hopes is Mankind vexed;

The Book of Life shows margin more than text.
Ecclesiastes and our glands agree:
A time for love, for work, for sleep, for tea.
Organic drumbeats score our ancient nerves:
Hark to their rhythms, conform to their curves.

All wrong? Advice, however sound, depends
Upon a meliorism Truth upends;
A certain Sinkingness resides in things.
The restless heart rejects what Fortune brings;
The Ego, too athletic, grows perverse
And muscle-builds by choosing worse and worse.
Our bones are prison-bars, our flesh is cells:
Where Suicide invites, Death-wish impels.
Earthquake, Diseases, Floods, Eruptions, Drought,
Black Comets, Starry Landslides, Wreck and Rout—
Beneath a cliff of vast Indifference
We light our frail fires, peg our poor tents.
The sleepless mouse-gray hours gnaw and stress:
"The Wisdom of the Earth is Foolishness."
Yet morning here, by Chilmark Pond, is fair.
The water scintillates against the air,
The grassy Earth spins seed from solar rage,
And patiently denies its awful age.
I am another world, no doubt; no doubt
We come into this World from well without.
The seasons lessen; Summer's touch betrays
A tired haste, a cool Autumnal trace.
The playground dust was richer, once, than loam,
And green, green as Eden, the slow path home.
No snows have been as deep as those my sled
Caressed to ice before I went to bed.
Perhaps Senility will give me back
The primitive rapport I lately lack.
Adulthood has its comforts: these entail
Sermons and sex and receipt of the mail,

Elimination's homely paean, dreams'
Mad gaiety, avoidance of extremes,
The friendship of children, the trust of banks,
Thoracic pangs, a stiffness in the shanks,
Foretastes of death, the aftertaste of sin,
In Winter, Whiskey, and in Summer, Gin.
   The marsh gives way to Pond, to Dunes, to Sea;
Cicadas call it good, and I agree.
At midpoint, center of a Hemisphere
Too blue for words, I've grown to love it here.
Earth wants me, it shall have me, yet not yet;
Some task remains, whose weight I can't forget,
Some package, anciently addressed, of praise,
That keeps me knocking on the doors of days.
   The time is gone, when *Pope* could ladle Wit
In couplet droplets, and decanter it.
Wordsworth's sweet brooding, *Milton*'s pride,
And *Tennyson*'s unease have all been tried;
Fin-de-siècle sickliness became
High-stepping Modernism, then went lame.
Art offers now, not cunning and exile,
But blank explosions and a hostile smile.
   Deepest in the thicket, thorns spell a word.
Born laughing, I've believed in the Absurd,
Which brought me this far; henceforth, if I can,
I must impersonate a serious man.

April–August 1968

LIVING WITH A WIFE

At the Piano

Barefoot in purple pants
and my ski sweater you
play the piano most seriously
Mozart fumbled with a grimace
the lamplight fumbling unfelt
in the down of your neck

Kind field from which my progeny
have fled to grow voices and fangs
you are an arena where art
like a badly killed bull swerves again

Your bare foot lifts
the lamplight pedals on
my house is half music
my wife holds no harm

In the Tub

You are a pond mirroring
pink clouds there is moss
where your white roots meet
when you lift your arm to shave
you are a younger kind of tree

Silver you rise from the lead
your swan arm seeks a towel
magic has taken place because
my Excalibur razor is dull
and the water would boil a man

Under the Sunlamp

Neuter your hair tugged back
harshly your face a shield
of greased copper less sexy
than a boy by Donatello
too bright to look at long
eyelids sealed in *Urfreude*
metal locked in blinding earth

During Menstruation

My house is on fire red
pain flickers on the walls wet
flame runs downstairs eggs
are hurled unripe from the furnace
and a frown hurts like smoke

Help I am sliding my cry
stands helpless as Galileo
at the side of moons revolving
of unwinding novae burning
flinging Tampax tubes of ash

All the While

Upstairs to my downstairs
echo to my silence
you walk through my veins shopping
and spin food from my sleep

*

I hear your small noises
you hide in closets without handles
you surprise me from the cellar
your foot-soles bright black

You slip in and out of beauty
and imply that nothing is wrong
Who sent you?
What is your assignment?

Though years sneak by like children
you stay as unaccountable
as the underwear set to soak
in the bowl where I brush my teeth

TOSSING AND TURNING

The spirit has infinite facets, but the body
confiningly few sides.
                                                    There is the left,
the right, the back, the belly, and tempting
in-betweens, northeasts and northwests,
that tip the heart and soon pinch circulation
in one or another arm.
                                                    Yet we turn each time
with fresh hope, believing that sleep
will visit us here, descending like an angel
down the angle our flesh's sextant sets,
tilted toward that unreachable star
hung in the night between our eyebrows, whence
dreams and good luck flow.
                                                            Uncross
your ankles. Unclench your philosophy.
This bed was invented by others; know we go
to sleep less to rest than to participate
in the twists of another world.
This churning is our journey.
                                                            It ends,
can only end, around a corner
we do not know
                                    we are turning.

ON AN ISLAND

Islanded, my wife turned on the radio for news of home.
Instead she heard that near us a plane had crashed into the sea.

She told me after dinner she couldn't face the flight home:
"What would I tell the children as we go down?"

I pooh-poohed her of course, said the odds were against it;
we made love with a desperate undercurrent, and fell asleep.

Then I awoke in the dark, and her fears appeared real.
The blinds were tilted back, my sunburn hurt, I was thirsty.

The tranquil ocean was yet enormous in its noise;
its hissing pursued me into each of the rooms.

My children were asleep, each small mouth darkly open;
"The radio said that a couple with a ten-year-old child

was found in the water, their bodies still clutching him."
Moonlight, pale as a moth, chasmed the front room with shadow

and lay white on the water, white on the sliding,
the huge-shushing sliding from island to island—

sleepless, inanimate, bottomless, prayer-denying,
the soughing of matter cast off by the sun, blind sun

among suns, massed liquid of atoms that conceives
and consumes, that communes with itself only,

soulless and mighty; our planes, our islands sink:
a still moon plates the sealed spot where they were.

MARCHING THROUGH A NOVEL

Each morning my characters
    greet me with misty faces
willing, though chilled, to muster
    for another day's progress
through the dazzling quicksand,
    the marsh of blank paper.
With instant obedience
    they change clothes and mannerisms,
drop a speech impediment,
    develop a motive backwards
to suit the deed that's done.
    They extend skeletal arms
for the handcuffs of contrivance,
    slog through docilely
maneuvers of coincidence,
    look toward me hopefully,
their general and quartermaster,
    for a clearer face, a bigger heart.
I do what I can for them,
    but it is not enough.
Forward is my order,
    though their bandages unravel
and some have no backbones
    and some turn traitor
like heads with two faces
    and some fall forgotten
in the trenchwork of loose threads,
    poor puffs of cartoon flak.
Forward. Believe me, I love them
    though I march them to finish them off.

THREE POEMS FROM AIRPLANES

Commuter Hop

People like living around lakes:
curved lines of houses, neat as teeth,
have gnawed the land near water bare.

The rest is woods.
The earth has mange.
How ungreen it is!—

though this is Connecticut, and April.
Pale spring like mildew grazes
the diagrams of baseball diamonds,

the tessellation of parking lots,
the necklaces of square-cut homes
left lying before blue mirrors.

Above What God Sees

God surely sees
from beneath the clouds
and never rises so high
men are invisible.
But here I have been lifted
to where a second horizon
delimits an Antarctica,
blue-veined terrain
where unnamed Obs and Lenas hang
unflowing, chasms roofed with glass
and static mountains shoulder
into horizontal sunlight Earth
cannot impinge upon.
The softness is motherly.
The truth is blasphemous
and pure. I remember
as if it were erotica

(with that same delicate dread
of its coming too true)
the unbelievable *livre*,
the flatland underneath:
red roofs, green fields
so bluntly and naïvely *there* you feel
the moist breath
of the child bent earnestly close
above the page
with his crayons.

Night Flight, over Ocean

Sweet fish tinned in the innocence of sleep,
we passengers together navigate
the firmament's subconscious-colored deep,
streaming aligned toward a landlocked gate.
Schooled (in customs, in foreign coin), from zone
to zone we slip, each clutching at the prize
(a camera, a seduction) torn from some lone
shore lost in our brains like the backs of our eyes.
Nationless, nowhere, we dream the ocean
we motionless plummet above, fuel roaring,
and stewardesses padding, and stray yen
or shillings jingling in the sky of our snoring.
Incipient, we stir; we burgeon, blank
dim swimmers borne toward the touchdown spank.

PHENOMENA

The tide goes up and down in the creek.
I wake each morning to witness
the black-clay banks bared like senile gums
or the marsh eclipsed by a second sky.

My furnace went out.
The man who fixed it let me look
at the rejuvenated flame;
it was astonishing.
In a cave of asbestos a vivid elf
went *dancy, dancy, dancy;*
his fingers and feet were uncountable;
he was all hot eye
and merry, so merry he roared.

I handle stones.
They like, perhaps, being handled.
In the earth, at the shovel's first strike,
they are mysterious—one might be
the tip of a China-sized cathedral.
But grubbing and cunning and cursing
bring them one by one to light,
disappointing when dried in the sun,
yet *there,* waterproof, fireproof,
dull veins disclosing a logic of form
and formation, but endurance the foremost quality.
I pile them; I alter their position in the universe.
By a tissue's-width difference, it matters.
Their surfaces say something to my hands.

At night, lying down, I cannot breathe.
A tree inside me clenches and I sweat.
There are reasons, there is medicine;
the frost of death
has found a chink in me, is all.

I breathe easier and, breathing, sleep.
The tide sighs and rises in my sleep.
The flame is furious in its cell below.
Under the moon the cold stones wait.

THE HOUSE GROWING

April 1972

The old house grows, adding rooms of silence.
My grandfather coughing as if to uproot
burdock from his lungs,
my grandmother tapping a ragged path
from duty to duty, and now
my father, prancing and whinnying
to dramatize his battle for the dollar,
pricking himself with pens to start each day—
all silent. The house grows vast.
Its windows take bites of the sky
to feed its flight toward emptiness. The mantel
restates its curve of molding undismayed;
the hearthstones fatten on the vanished.

APOLOGIES TO HARVARD

The Phi Beta Kappa Poem, 1973

Fair, square Harvard, crib of the pilgrim mind;
Home of the hermit scholar, who pursues
His variorums undistracted by
All riots, sensual or for a cause;
Vast village where the wise enjoy the young;
Refuge of the misshapen and unformed;
Stylistic medley (Richardson's stout brown,
Colonial scumble, Puseyite cement,
And robber-baron Gothic pile their slates
In floating soot, beneath house-tower domes
The playtime polychrome of M & Ms);
Fostering mother: time, that doth dissolve
Granite like soap and dries to bone all tears,
Devoured my quartet of student years
And, stranger still, the twenty minus one
Since I was hatched and certified your son.

A generation steeped in speed and song,
In Doctor Spock, TV, and denim *chic*
Has come and gone since, Harvard, we swapped vows
And kept them—mine, to grease the bursar's palm,
To double-space submitted work, to fill
All bluebooks set before me (spilling ink
As avidly as puppies lap a bowl
Till empty of the blankness of the milk),
To wear a tie and jacket to my meals,
To drop no water bags from windows, nor
Myself (though *Werther*, Kierkegaard, and *Lear*
All sang the blues, the deans did not, and warned
That suicide would constitute a blot
Upon one's record), to obey the rules
Yclept "parietal" (as if the walls, not I,
Were guilty if a girl were pinched between
Them after ten); in short, to strive, to bear,
To memorize my notes, to graduate:
These were my vows. Yours were, in gourmet terms,

To take me in, raw as I was, and chew
And chew and chew for one quadrennium,
And spit me out, by God, a gentleman.
We did our bits. All square, and no regrets.
On my side, little gratitude; but why?
So many other men—the founding race
Of farmer-divines, the budding Brahmins
Of Longfellow's time, the fragile sprats
Of fortunes spun on sweatshop spindles
Along the Merrimack, the golden crew
Of raccoon-coated hip-flask-swiggers and
Ritz-tea-dance goers, the continual tribe
Of the studious, the smart, and the shy—
Had left their love like mortar 'twixt your bricks,
Like sunlight synthesized within your leaves,
Had made your morning high noon of their days
And clung, there seemed no need for me to stay.
I came and paid, a trick, and stole away.

The Fifties—Cold War years *par excellence*—
Loom in memory's mists as an iceberg, slow
In motion and sullenly radiant.
I think, those years, it often snowed because
My freshman melancholy took the print
Of a tread-marked boot in slush, crossing to Latin
With Cerberean Dr. Havelock
In Sever 2, or to Lamont's Math 1
With some tall nameless blameless section man
To whom the elegant was obvious,
Who hung Greek letters on his blackboard curves
Like trinkets on a Christmas tree and who
I hope is happy in Schenectady,
Tending toward zero, with children my age then
To squint confused into his lucent mind.
There was a taste of coffee and of cold.
My parents' house had been a hothouse world
Of complicating, inward-feeding jokes.
Here, wit belonged to the dead; the wintry smiles

Of snowmen named Descartes and Marx and Milton
Hung moonlit in the blizzards of our brains.
Homesick, I walked to class with eyes downcast
On heelprints numberless as days to go.

And when bliss came, as it must to sophomores,
Snow toppled still, but evening-tinted mauve,
Exploding on the windows of the Fogg
Like implorations of a god locked out
While we were sealed secure inside, in love,
Or coolly close—but close enough, we felt,
To make a life or not, as chances willed.
Meanwhile there were cathedral fronts to know
And cigarettes to share—our breaths straight smoke—
And your bicycle, snickering, to wheel
Along the wet diagonal of the walk
That led Radcliffewards through the snowy Yard.
Kiss, kiss, the flakes surprised our faces; *oh*,
The arching branches overhead exclaimed,
Gray lost in gray like limestone ribs at Rheims;
Wow-ow!—as in a comic-strip balloon
A siren overstated its alarm,
Bent red around a corner hurtling toward
Extragalactic woe, and left behind
Our blue deserted world of silent storm.
Tick, tick-a, tick-a, tick, your bike spokes spake
Well-manneredly, not wishing to impose
Their half-demented repetitious thoughts
Upon your voice, or mine: what *did* we say?
Your voice was like your skin, an immanence,
A latent tangency that swelled my cells,
Young giant deafened by my whirling size.
And in your room—brave girl, you had a room,
You were a woman, with inner space to fill,
Leased above Sparks Street, higher than a cloud—
Water whistled itself to tea, cups clicked,
Your flaxen flat-mate's quick Chicago voice
Incited us to word games, someone typed,

The telephone and radio checked in
With bulletins, and, nicest noise of all,
All noises died, the snow kept silent watch,
The slanting back room private as a tent
Resounded with the rustle of our blood,
The susurration of surrendered clothes.

We took the world as given. Cigarettes
Were twenty-several cents a pack, and gas
As much per gallon. Sex came wrapped in rubber
And veiled in supernatural scruples—call
Them chivalry. A certain breathlessness
Was felt; perhaps the Bomb, which first proclaimed
*Mu*SHROOM! just as we entered puberty,
Waking us from the newspaper-nightmare
Our childhoods had napped through, was realer then;
Our lives, at least, were not assumed to be
Our right; we lived, by shifts, on sufferance.
The world contained policemen, true, and these
Should be avoided. Governments were bunk,
But well-intentioned. Blacks were beautiful
But seldom met. The poor were with ye always.
We thought one war as moral as the next,
Believed that life was tragic and absurd,
And were absurdly cheerful, just like Sartre.
We loved John Donne and Hopkins, Yeats and Pound,
Plus all things convolute and dry and pure.
Medieval history was rather swank;
Psychology was in the mind; abstract
Things grabbed us where we lived; the only life
Worth living was the private life; and—last,
Worst scandal in this characterization—
We did not know we were a generation.

Forgive us, Harvard; Royce and William James
Could not construe a Heaven we could reach.
We went forth, married young, and bred like mink.
We seized what jobs the System offered, raked

Our front yards, stayed together for the kids,
And chalked up meekly as a rail-stock-holder
Each year's depreciation of our teeth,
Our skin-tone, hair, and confidence. The white
Of Truman's smile and Eisenhower's brow
Like mildew furs our hearts. The possible
Is but a suburb, Harvard, of your city.
Seniors, come forth; we crave your wrath and pity.

HEADING FOR NANDI

Out of Honolulu
heading for Nandi
I ask them, "Where's Nandi?"
The man tells me, "Fiji."

The airport is open
the night sky black panels
between cement pillars.
I wish I had a woman.

Around me Australians
are holding hands matily
as back in Waikiki
the honeymooners strolled.

By daylight bikinis
strolled bare on the pavement
the honeymoon brides
with waists white as milk

and the Japanese couples
posed each for the other
the women as dainty
as self-painted dolls

and the watching Polynesians
laughed quick as Fayaway
dark as cooking chocolate
that always tasted bitter

and the haunted Americans
with flatland accents
in plastic leis wandered
the blue streets of love.

From the taxi I witnessed
two men embracing

embracing and crying.
I assumed they were sailors.

Nandi? I'll see it
or die in these hours
that face me like panels
in a chapel by Rothko.

I wish I had a woman
to touch me or tell me
she is frightened to go there
or would be, but for me.

GOLFERS

One-gloved beasts in cleats, they come clattering
down to the locker room in bogus triumph, bulls
with the *pics* of their pars still noisy in them,
breathing false fire of stride, strike, stride, and putt.
We dread them, their brown arms and rasp of money,
their slacks the colors of ice cream, their shoes,
whiter than bones, that stipple the downtrodden green
and take an open stance on the backs of the poor.

Breathing of bourbon, crowing, they strip:
the hair of their chests is grizzled, their genitals
hang dead as practice balls, their blue legs twist;
where, now, are their pars and their furor?
Emerging from the shower shrunken, they are men,
mere men, old boys, lost, the last hole a horror.

POISONED IN NASSAU

By the fourth (or is it the fifth?)
day, one feels poisoned—by
last night's rum, this morning's sun,
the tireless pressure of leisure.

The sea's pale green seems evil.
The shells seem pellets, the meals
forced doses, Bahamian cooking
as bitterly obsequious as
the resentful wraiths that serve it.

Vertigo is reading at the beach
words a thousand miles away,
is tasting Coppertone again,
is closing one's eyes once more against
the mismatch of poverty and beauty.

The beautiful sea is pale, it is
sick, its fish sting like regrets.
Perhaps it was the conch salad, or is
the something too rich in Creation.

LEAVING CHURCH EARLY

What, I wonder, were we hurrying to,
my grandfather, father, mother, myself,
as the last anthem was commencing? Were
we avoiding the minister's hand at the door?
My mother shied, in summer, from being touched.
Or was it my father, who thought life was grim
and music superfluous, dodging the final hymn?
Or could, I wonder now, the impetus
that moved the small procession of us up
and out, apologizing, from the pew
have come from the ancient man, mysterious
to me as an ancestor turned to ash,
who held some thunders though, a tavern bully
in his time and still a steadfast disliker
of other people's voices? Whatever the cause,
we moved, *bump* and whisper, down
the side aisle, while the organ mulled Stanza One,
a quadruped herd, branded as kin, I
the last of the line, adolescent, a-blush,
out through the odor of piety and the scents
(some purchased at Kresge's, some given by God)
my buxom country cousins harbored in
their cotton dresses, to the sighing exit
which opened on the upbeat as the choir
in love of the Lord and imperfect unison
flung its best self over the balcony.

The lifted voices drifted behind us, spurned.
Loose pebbles acknowledged our shoes.
Our Buick, black and '36, was parked
in a hickory picnic grove where a quoit stake,
invisible as Satan in the grass
of Eden, might spear a tire "of the unwary,"
as my grandfather put it. The interior
of the auto hit us with an hour's heat.
We got in gear, our good clothes mussed,
and, exonerated for the week, bounced home.

*

Home: the fields, red, with acid rows of corn
and sandstone corner-markers. The undertone
of insect-hum, the birds too full to sing.
A Sunday haze in Pennsylvania.
My unchurched grandma stoops in the foursquare house,
as we prattle in the door, like a burglar
trapped in mid-theft, half-paralyzed, her frame
hung in my memory between two tasks,
about to do something, but what? A cream
jug droops in her hand, empty or it would spill—
or is it a potato-masher, or
a wooden spoon? White-haired, stricken, she stares
and to welcome us back searches for a word.

What had we hurried back to? There could be
no work: a mock-Genesiac rest reigned
in the bewitched farmland. Our strawberries
rotted in their rows unrummaged-for;
no snorting, distant tractor underlined
the rasp of my father's pencil as he marked,
with his disappointed grimace, math exams.
The dogs smelled boredom, and collapsed their bones.
The colors of the Sunday comics jangled,
printed off-key, and my grandfather's feet,
settling in for a soliloquy, kicked up fuzz.
My father stood to promenade his wounds.
I lay down, feeling weak, and pulled a book
across my eyes the way a Bedouin
in waiting out a sandstorm drapes his sheet.
The women clucked and quarrelled with the pots
over who was cook. A foody fog
arose. The dogs rose with it, and the day
looked as if it might survive to noon.

What is wrong with this picture? What is strange?
Each figure tends its own direction, keeps

the axis of its own theatric chore,
scattered, anarchic, kept home by poverty,
with nowhere else to go. A modern tribe
would be aligned around "the television,"
the family show-off, the sparkling prodigy
that needs a constant watching lest it sulk and cease
to lift into celebrity the arc
of interlocked anonymous: we were not such.
We spurned all entertainment but our misery.
"Jesus," my father cried, "I hate the world!"
"Mother," my mother called, "you're in the way!"
"Be grateful for your blessings," Grandpa advised,
shifting his feet and showing a hairless shin.
"*Ach*," Grandma brought out in self-defense,
the syllable a gem of German indignation,
its guttural edge unchipped, while I,
still in the sabbath shirt and necktie, bent
my hopes into the latest Nero Wolfe, imagining
myself orchidaceous in Manhattan and
mentally constructing, not Whodunit,
but How to Get Out of Here: my dastardly plot.

The rug, my closest friend, ignored
my jabbing elbows. Geraniums raged on the sills.
The furniture formed a living dismal history
of heritage, abandonment, and purchase,
pretension, compromise, and wear: the books
tried to believe in a better world but failed.
An incongruous painting told of dunes
and a dab of unattainable sea.
Outside, a lone car passed; the mailbox held
no hope of visitation—no peacock magazine,
wrapped in brown paper, rife with ads, would come
to unremind us of what we were, poor souls
who had left church early to be about
the business of soaking ourselves in Time,
dunking doughnuts let fall into the cup.
Hot Pennsylvania, hazy, hugged the walls

of sandstone two feet thick as other cells
enfold the carcinomic hyperactive one; we were
diseased, unneighborly, five times alone, and quick.

What was our hurry? Sunday afternoon
beckoned with radioed ball games, soft ice cream,
furtive trips in the creaking auto, naps
for the elderly, daydreams for the young,
while blind growth steamed to the horizon of hills,
the Lord ignoring His own injunction to rest.
My book grew faint. My grandfather lifted his head,
attentive to what he alone divined;
his glasses caught the light, his nose
reclaimed an ancient handsomeness.
His wife, wordless, came and sat beside.
My father swished his hips within his bath of humor
and called his latest recognition to the other
co-captain of dissatisfaction; my mother
came to the living-room doorway, and told us off.
She is the captive, we are the clumsy princes
who jammed the casket with our bitter kisses.
She is our prison, the rampart of her forehead
a fiery red. We shake our chains, amused.
Her myths and our enactment tickle better
the underside of facts than Bible fables;
here to this house, this mythy *then*, we hurried,
dodging the benediction to bestow,
ourselves upon ourselves, the final word.

Envoi

My mother, only you remember with me—
you alone still populate that room.
You write me cheerful letters mentioning Cher
and Barbara Walters as if they were there with you,
realer than the dead. We left church early
why? To talk? To love? To eat? To be free

of the world's crass consensus? Now you read,
you write me, Aristotle and Tolstoy
and claim to be amazed, how much they knew.
I send you this poem as my piece of the puzzle.
We know the truth of it, the past, how strange,
how many corners wouldn't bear describing,
the angles of it, how busy we were forgiving—
we had no time, of course, we *have* no time
to do all the forgiving that we must do.

ANOTHER DOG'S DEATH

For days the good old bitch had been dying, her back
pinched down to the spine and arched to ease the pain,
   her kidneys dry, her muzzle white. At last
I took a shovel into the woods and dug her grave

in preparation for the certain. She came along,
which I had not expected. Still, the children gone,
   such expeditions were rare, and the dog,
spayed early, knew no nonhuman word for love.

She made her stiff legs trot and let her bent tail wag.
We found a spot we liked, where the pines met the field.
   The sun warmed her fur as she dozed and I dug;
I carved her a safe place while she protected me.

I measured her length with the shovel's long handle;
she perked in amusement, and sniffed the heaped-up earth.
   Back down at the house, she seemed friskier,
but gagged, eating. We called the vet a few days later.

They were old friends. She held up a paw, and he
injected a violet fluid. She swooned on the lawn;
   we watched her breathing quickly slow and cease.
In the wheelbarrow up to the hole, her fur took the sun.

DREAM AND REALITY

I am in a room.
Everything is white, the walls
are white, there are no windows.
There is a door.
I open it, and neatly
as a shadow a coating of snow
falls door-shaped into the room.
I think, *Snow,* not surprised
it is inside and outside both,
as with an igloo.
I move through the open door
into the next room; this, too, is
white and windowless and perfect.
I think, *There must be more than this.*
This is a dream.

My daughter finds bones
on the marshes. I examine them:
deer heads with sockets round as
cartoon eyes, slender jaws broken.
There are tiny things, too,
no bigger than a pulled tooth,
and just that white—burrs of bone,
intricate, with pricking flanges
where miniature muscles attached.
She says, *Those are mouse jaws.*
Indeed: I see teeth like rows
of the letter "i" in diamond type.
She tells me, *I find them*
in the cough balls of owls.
And this is reality.

DUTCH CLEANSER

My grandmother used it, Dutch Cleanser,
in the dark Shillington house,
in the kitchen darkened by the grape arbor,
and I was frightened of the lady on the can.
Why was she carrying a stick?
Why couldn't we see her face?

Now I, an aging modern man,
estranged, alone, and medium gray,
I tip Dutch Cleanser onto a sponge,
here in this narrow bathroom,
where the ventilator fan has to rumble
when all I want to switch on is light.

The years have spilled since Shillington,
the daily *Eagle*s stacked in the closet
have burst the roof! Look up,
Deutsche Grossmutter—I am here!
You have changed, I have changed,
Dutch Cleanser has changed not at all.

The lady is still upholding the stick
chasing dirt, and her face
is so angry we dare not see it.
The dirt she is chasing is ahead of her,
around the can, like a minute hand
the hour hand pushes around.

RATS

A house has rotten places: cellar walls
where mud replaces mortar every rain,
the loosening board that begged for nails in vain,
the sawed-off stairs, and smelly nether halls
the rare repairman never looks behind
and if he did would, disconcerted, find
long spaces, lathed, where dead air grows a scum
of fuzz, and rubble deepens crumb by crumb.

Here they live. Hear them on their boulevards
beneath the attic flooring tread the shards
of panes from long ago, and Fiberglas
fallen to dust, and droppings, and dry clues
to crimes no longer news. The villains pass
with scrabbly traffic-noise; their avenues
run parallel to chambers of our own
where we pretend we're clean and all alone.

CALDER'S HANDS

In the little movie
at the Whitney
you can see them
at the center of the spell
of wire and metal:

a clumsy man's hands,
square and mitten-thick,
that do everything
without pause:
unroll a tiny rug

with a flick,
tug a doll's arm up,
separate threads:
these hands now dead
never doubted, never rested.

SPANISH SONNETS

I.

By the light of insomnia, truths
that by daylight don't look so bad—
one is over the hill, will die, and has
an appointment tomorrow that can't be broken—
become a set of slippery caves.
Bare facts that cast no shadow at noon
echo and shudder, swallow and loom.
To be alive is to be mad.

Can it be? Only Goya pictures it.
Those last brown paintings smeared in Madrid
fill a room with insomnia's visions,
a Spanish language rapid as a curse.
Prayer's a joke, love a secretion;
the tortured torture, and worse gets worse.

II.

He omits, Goya, not even the good news:
the pink-cheeked peasants in the ideal open,
the village health, the ring of children,
in days when everyone dressed like lords.
Carlos the Fourth wears a fool's mild smile,
and the royal family, a row of breeders,
are softly human, and in this style still
the white-shirted rebel throws up his arms.

The red scream darkens, the brushstrokes plunge
headlong into Rouault, where evil
faces are framed like saints' by lead.
The astonishing *Half-Hidden Dog*
for a sky has a Turner. Pain is paint
and people are meat, as for Francis Bacon.

III.

Yes, self-obsession fills our daily clothes,
bulges them outward like armor,
but at night self must be shed,
the room must be hollow, each lamp
and table crazily exact, and the door
snug in the frame of its silence. When we
can imagine the room when we are not there,
we are asleep. The world hasn't ended.

I worry for you a hemisphere away,
awaiting the edge of evening while I,
deep in midnight, plump the pillow,
turn on the light, and curse the clock.
The planet's giant motion overpowers us.
We cannot stop clinging where we are.

IV.

Each day's tour, I gather sandy castles,
cathedrals of marzipan gone bad,
baroque exploding sunbursts in Toledo,
filigreed silver crosses in Ávila,
like magnified mold proliferating.
The tragical stink of old religion—
greasy-eyed painters trying too hard,
crucifix-carvers gone black in the thumb.

And the Moor piled up brick and ochre,
and the Christian nailed iron in turn
to the gates of the city, and the land breathes green
under power lines hung upon windmills,
and I try to picture your body part by part
to supplant the day's crenellated loot.

V.

The land is dry enough to make the rivers
dramatic here. You say you love me;
as the answer to your thirst, I splash,
fall, and flow, a varied cool color.
Here fountains celebrate intersections,
and our little Fiats eddy and whirl
on the way to siesta and back.
They say don't drink tap water, but I do.

Unable to sleep, I make water at night
to lighten myself for a phantom trip.
My image in the mirror is undramatic,
merely old and nude—a wineskin.
Who could ever love me? Misread
road maps pour out of me in a stream.

VI.

Neumático punturado—we stopped
on the only empty spot in Spain,
a concrete stub road forgotten between
a steep grass slope up to an orange wall
and a froth of mustard veiling two poppies.
Blessedly, the native space held back,
the Fiat held mute while we puzzled through
its code of metal to the spare and the jack.

¡Milagro! It rose like a saint, the car,
on a stiff sunbeam; nuts fell from the wheel
with the ease of bread breaking. The change
achieved, we thankfully looked up. Three men
in sky-blue work clothes in a sky of green
in silence wielded sickles. They had seen.

VII.

All crises pass, though not the condition of crisis.
Today I saw Franco as a bookend, with Juan Carlos.
The king is much on television, and indeed
seems telegenic. Slept well last night,
with dreams in deeper colors than there are.
Imagine a cardinal's biscuit palace, friable,
from whose uncountable windows peep
hospital bedsteads painted lime-green:

I saw this in sunlight. The people
are clean, white, courteous, industrious.
To buy an inner tube, pay a traffic fine,
order Cinzano—this is civilization.
The streets, though dim, are safe at night. Lovers
touch, widows wear black, all is known.

VIII.

These islands of history amid traffic snarls—
Joanna the Mad in Tordesillas
played the harpsichord, leaned on the parapet,
saw a river, great fields, a single man
hooking a sheep who had gone the wrong way;
in Valladolid, Alvaro de Luna
knelt in the tiny, now dirty plaqued plaza
called Ochavo to be beheaded.

These souls thought the stars heaved with them.
My life has seamed shut; I sleep
as return to you dawns like a comet.
Rubber tires burn where martyrs bled,
the madness of sunshine melts the plain,
tulips outnumber truths in my Madrid.

TO ED SISSMAN

I.

I think a lot about you, Ed:
tell me why. Your sallow owlish face
with the gray wart where death had kissed it,
drifting sideways above your second gin
in Josèph's, at lunch, where with a what-the-hell
lurch you had commanded the waiter
to bring more poison, hangs in my mind
as a bloated star I wish to be brave on.

I loved your stuff, and the way
it came from nowhere, where poetry
must come from, having no credentials.
Your talk was bland, with a twist of whine,
of the obvious man affronted. You stooped
more and more, shouldering the dark for me.

II.

When you left, the ceiling caved in.
The impossible shrank to the plausible.
In that final room, where one last book
to be reviewed sat on your chest, you said,
like an incubus, transparent tubes
moved in and out of your veins
and nurses with volleyball breasts
mocked us with cheerleader health.

You were sicker than I, but I huddled in
my divorcing man's raincoat by your bed
like a drenched detective by the cozy fire
a genial suspect has laid in his manor,
unsuspecting he is scheduled Next Victim.
I mourned I could not solve the mystery.

III.

You told me, lunching at Josèph's,
foreseeing death, that it would be
a comfort to believe. My faith,
a kind of rabbit frozen in the headlights,
scrambled for cover in the roadside brush
of gossip; your burning beams passed by.
"Receiving communications from beyond": thus
you once described the fit of writing well.

The hint hangs undeveloped, like
my mental note to send you Kierkegaard.
Forgive me, Ed; no preacher, I—
a lover of the dust, like you,
who took ten years of life on trial
and gave pentameter another voice.

ON THE WAY TO DELPHI

Oedipus slew his father near this muddy field
the bus glides by as it glides by many another,
and Helicon is real; the Muses hid and dwelled
on a hill, less than a mountain, that we could climb
if the bus would stop and give us the afternoon.

From these small sites, now overrun by roads and fame,
dim chieftains stalked into the world's fog and grew huge.
Where shepherds sang their mistaken kings, stray factories
mar with cement and smoke the lean geology
that wants to forget—*has* forgotten—the myths it bred.

We pass stone slopes where houses, low, of stone, blend in
like utterings on the verge of sleep—accretions scarce
distinguishable from scree, on the uphill way
to architecture and law. No men are visible.
All out: Parnassus. The oracle's voice is wild.

CRAB CRACK

In the Pond

The blue crabs come to the brown pond's edge
to browse for food where the shallows are warm
and small life thrives subaqueously,
while we approach from the airy side,
great creatures bred in trees and armed
with nets on poles of such a length
as to outreach that sideways tiptoe lurch
when, with a splash from up above, the crabs
discover themselves to be prey.

In the Bucket

We can feel
at the pole's other end their fearful
wide-legged kicking, like the fury of scissors
if scissors had muscle. We want
their sweet muscle. Blue and a multitude
of colors less easily named (scum-green,
old ivory, odd ovals of lipstick-red
where the blue-glazed limbs are hinged),
they rest in the buckets, gripping one another
feebly, like old men fumbling in their laps,
numb with puzzlement, their brains
a few threads, each face a mere notch
on the brittle bloated pancake of the carapace.

In the Pot

But the passion with which they resist!
Even out of the boiling pot they come clattering
and try to dig holes in the slick kitchen floor
and flee as if hours parching in the sun
on the lawn beneath our loud cocktails
had not taught them a particle of despair.

On the Table

Now they are done, red. Cracking
their preposterous backs, we cannot bear
to touch the tender fossils of their mouths
and marvel at the beauty of the gills,
the sweetness of the swimmerets. All is exposed,
an intricate toy. Life spins such miracles
by multiples of millions, yet our hearts
never quite harden, never quite cease

to look for the hand of mercy in
such workmanship. If when we die we're dead,
then the world is ours like gaudy grain
to be reaped while we're here, without guilt.
If not, then an ominous duty to feel
with the mite and the dragon is ours,
and a burden in being.

In the Stomach

Late at night
the ghosts of the crabs patrol our intestines,
scampering sideways, hearkening *à pointe*
like radar dishes beneath the tide, seeking
the safe grave of sand in vain, turning,
against their burning wills, into us.

THE MOONS OF JUPITER

Callisto, Ganymede, Europa, Io:
these four, their twinkling spied by Galileo
in his new-invented telescope, debunked
the dogma of celestial spheres—great bubbles
of crystal turning one within another,
our pancake Earth the static, sea-rimmed center,
and, like a beehive, Purgatory hung below,
and angels scattered all throughout, chiming
and trumpeting across the curved interstices
their glad and constant news. Not so. "*E pur
si muove*," Galileo muttered, *sotto
voce*, having recanted to the Pope.

Yet, it moves, the Earth, and unideal
also the Galilean moons: their motion
and fluctuant occlusions pierced Jove's sphere
and let out all the air that Dante breathed
as tier by singing tier he climbed to where
Beatrice awaited, frosting bride
atop the universal wedding cake.
Not Vergil now but Voyager, cloned gawker
sent spinning through the asymptotic skies
and televising back celestial news,
guides us to the brink of the bearable.

Callisto is the outermost satellite
and the first our phantom footsteps tread.
Its surface underfoot is ancient ice,
thus frozen firm four billion years ago
and chipped and peppered since into a slurry
of saturated cratering. Pocked, knocked,
and rippled sullenly, this is the terrain
of unforgiven wrongs and hurts preserved—
the unjust parental slap, the sneering note
passed hand to hand in elementary school,
the sexual jibe confided between cool sheets,
the bad review, the lightly administered snub.
All, in this gloom, keep jagged edges fresh

as yesterday, and, muddied by some silicon,
the bitter spikes and uneroded rims
of ancient impact trip and lacerate
our progress. There is no horizon, just
widespread proof of ego's cruel bombardment.

Next, Ganymede, the largest of these moons,
as large as toasted Mercury. Its ice enchants
with ponds where we can skate and peek down through
pale recent crazings to giant swarthy flakes
of mineral mystery; raked blocks like glaciers
must be traversed, and vales of strange grooves cut
by a parallel sliding, implying
tectonic activity, a once-warmed interior.
This is the realm of counterthrust—the persistent
courtship, the job application, the punch
given back to the ribs of the opposing tackle.
A rigid shame attends these ejecta,
and a grim satisfaction we did not go under
meekly, but thrust our nakedness hard
against the skin of the still-fluid world,
leaving what is called here a ghost crater.

"Cue ball of the satellites"—so joked
the *National Geographic* of Europa.
But, landed on the fact, the mind's eye swims
in something somber and delicious both—
a merged Pacific and Siberia,
an opalescent prairie veined with beige
and all suffused by flickers of a rose
tint caught from great, rotating Jupiter.
Europa's surface stretches still and smooth,
so smooth its horizon's glossy limb betrays
an arc of curvature. The meteors here
fell on young flesh and left scars
no deeper than birthmarks; as we walk
our chins are lit from underneath, the index
of reflection, the albedo, is so high.

Around us glares the illusion of success:
a certain social polish, decent grades,
accreditations, memberships, applause,
and mutual overlookings melt together
to form one vast acceptance that makes us blind.

On Io, volcanoes plume, and sulphur tugged
by diverse gravitations bubbles forth
from a golden crust that caps a molten sea.
The atmosphere smells foul, and pastel snow
whips burningly upon us, amid the cold.
This is our heart, our bowels, ever renewed,
the poisonous churn of basic needs
suffering the pull of bodies proximate.
The bulblike limbic brain, the mother's breast,
the fear of death, the wish to kill, the itch
to plunge and flee, the love of excrement,
the running sore and appetitive mouth
all find form here. Kilometers away,
a melancholy puckered caldera
erupts, and magma, gas, and crystals hurl
toward outer space a smooth blue column that
umbrellas overhead—some particles
escaping Io's seething gravity.

Straining upward out of ourselves to follow
their flight, we confront the forgotten
witness, Jupiter's thunderous mass,
the red spot roaring like an anguished eye
amid a turbulence of boiling eyebrows—
an emperor demented but enthroned,
and hogging with his gases an empyrean
in which the Sun is just another star.
So, in a city, as we hurry along
or swiftly ascend to the sixtieth floor,
enormity suddenly dawns and we become
beamwalkers treading a hand's-breadth of steel,
the winds of space shining around our feet.

Striated by slow-motion tinted tumult
and lowering like a cloud, the planet turns,
vast ball, annihilating *other*,
epitome of ocean, mountain, cityscape
whose mass would crush us were we once
to stop the inward chant, *This is not real.*

UPON THE LAST DAY OF HIS FORTY-NINTH YEAR

Scritch, *scratch*, saith the frozen spring snow—
not near enough, this season or the last,
but still a skin for skiing on, with care.
At every shaky turn into the fall line
one hundred eighty pounds of tired blood
and innards weakly laced with muscle seek
to give themselves to gravity and ruin.
My knees, a-tremble with old reflex, resist
and try to find the lazy dancer's step
and pillowed curve my edges flirted with
when I had little children to amaze
and life seemed endlessly flexible. Now,
my heavy body swings to face the valley
and feels the gut pull of steep maturity.

SMALL-CITY PEOPLE

They look shabby and crazy but not
in the campy big-city way of those
who really would kill you or really do
have a million dollars in the safe at home—
dudes of the absolute, swells of the dark.

Small-city people hardly expect to get
looked at, in their parkas
and their hunting caps and babushkas
and Dacron suits and outmoded
bouffants. No tourists come
to town to stare, no Japanese
or roving photographers.

The great empty mills, the wide main drag
with its boarded-up display windows,
the clouded skies that never quite rain
form a rock there is no out from under.

The girls look tough, the men look tired,
the old people dress up for a circus called off
because of soot, and snarl
with halfhearted fury, their hats
on backwards. The genetic pool
confluxes to cast up a rare beauty,
or a boy full of brains:
these can languish as in a desert
or eventually flourish, for not being
exploited too soon.

Small cities are kind, for
failure is everywhere, ungrudging;
not to mention free parking
and bowls of little pretzels in the ethnic bars.
Small-city people know what they know,

and what they know is what you learn
only living in a place
no one would choose but that chose you,
flatteringly.

PLOW CEMETERY

The Plow: one of the three-mile inns that nicked
the roads that led to Reading and eased the way.
From this, Plow Hill, Plowville—a little herd
of sandstone, barn and house like cow and calf,
brown-sided—and, atop the hill, Plow Church,
a lumpy Lutheran pride whose bellied stones
Grandfather Hoyer as a young buck wheeled
in a clumsy barrow up the bending planks
that scaffolded around the rising spire.
He never did forget how those planks bent
beneath his weight conjoined with that of rock,
on high; he would tell of it in the tone
with which he recounted, to childish me,
dental pain he had endured. The drill,
the dentist warned him, would approach the nerve.
"And indeed it did approach it, very close!"
he said, with satisfaction, savoring
the epic taste his past had in his mouth.

What a view he must have commanded then,
the hickory handles tugging in his palms!—
the blue-brown hills, Reading a red-brick smudge
eleven winding miles away. The northward view
is spacious even from the cemetery,
Plow Cemetery, downhill from the church.
Here rest my maternal forebears underneath
erect or slightly tipping slender stones,
the earliest inscribed *Hier ruhe*, then
with arcs of sentimental English set
afloat above the still-Germanic names
in round relief the regional soft rock
releases to the air slow grain by grain
until the dates that framed a brisk existence
spent stamping amid animals and weather
are weathered into timelessness. Still sharp,
however, V-cut in imported granite,
stand shadowed forth John Hoyer's name, his wife's,
his daughter's, and his son-in-law's. All four

mar one slab as in life they filled one house,
my mother's final year left blank. Alert
and busy aboveground, she's bought a plot
for me—for *me*—in Plow Cemetery.

Our earth here is red, like blood mixed with flour,
and slices easy; my cousin could dig
a grave in a morning with pick and shovel.
Now his son, also my cousin, mounts
a backhoe, and the shuddering machine
quick-piles what undertakers, for the service,
cloak in artificial turf as tinny
as Christmas. New mounds weep pink in the rain.
Live moles hump up the porous, grassy ground.
Traffic along Route 10 is quieter now
the Interstate exists in parallel,
forming a four-lane S in the middle view
that wasn't there before, this side the smudge
red Reading makes between its blue-brown hills.
Except for this and ever-fresher graves,
all changes are organic here. At first,
I did resent my mother's heavy gift,
her plot to bring me home; but slowly I
have come to think, Why not? Where else? I will
have been away for fifty years, perhaps,
but have forever to make my absence up.
My life in time will seal shut like a scar.

STYLES OF BLOOM

One sudden week (the roads still salty,
and only garlic green) forsythia
shouts out in butter-yellow monotone
from hedge to hedge and yard to yard,
a shout the ochre that precedes
maple leaves echoes overhead.

The dogwood's blossoms float sideways
like stars in the dark that teatime brings
to the side of the tall brick house,
but almost vanish, melting flakes,
in morning's bald spring sun.

Lilac: an explosion of ego
odorous creamily, each raceme
dewy till noon, then overnight
turned papery and faded—a souvenir.

In arches weighed by fragile suds,
the bridal wreath looks drenched.
White as virtue is white, plain
as truth is plain, the bushes can't wait
to shed their fat bundles of sequins;
burdensome summer has come.

TWO HOPPERS

Displayed in the Thyssen-Bornemisza Collection

The smaller, older *Girl at a Sewing Machine*
   shows her, pale profile obscured by her hair,
at work beneath an orange wall while sky

in pure blue pillars stands in a window bay.
   She is alone and silent. The heroine
of *Hotel Room*, down to her slip, gazes

at a letter unfolded upon her naked knees.
   Her eyes and face are in shadow. The day
rumbles with invisible traffic outside

this room where a wall is yellow, where
   a bureau blocks our way with brown and luggage
stands in wait of its unpacking near

a green armchair: sun-wearied, Thirties plush.
   We have been here before. The slanting light,
the woman alone and held amid the planes

of paint by some mysterious witness we're
   invited to breathe beside. The sewing girl,
the letter. Hopper is saying, *I am Vermeer.*

THE CODE

Were there no rain there would be little noise,
no rustle on the roof that we confuse
with our own bloodbeat on the inner ear,
no braided gurgle in the gutter, no breathing
within the tree whose shelved and supple bulk
sifts the rain to a mist of small descents.

A visitor come from a cloudless planet
would stand amazed by the tumults of our water
and feel bereaved. Without the rain
the taxi wheels would pass like wind on sand
and all the splashing that excites our lovers
fresh from drinks would be a chastening calm;

the sky would be devoid of those enormous
witnesses who hang invisible
until our wish to see brings forth in focus
their sliding incandescent shapes.
Without the rain the very links of life
would drift still uncemented, a dream of dust.

Were there no rain the windowpanes
would never tick as if a spy outside,
who once conspired with us to ferret out
the secret code, the terms of full concord
with all that is and will be, were signalling
with a fingernail, *I'm back, I've got the goods.*

RICHMOND

The shadows in his eye sockets like shades
upon a bearded hippie, Stonewall Jackson
stares down Monument Avenue toward where Lee
sits on an even higher horse. The cause
was lost but lingers in the faintly defiant
dignity of the pale-gray, Doric dollhouse
from whence Jeff Davis, conscientious Satan,
directed our second rebellion: a damn good try.

Brick graciousness prevails; across the James
wood houses hold black pensioners, and Poe's
ghost haunts a set of scattered tombs, *musei*
exposing to Northern visitors his quills,
a model of his muddy city, and
an etching of, wry-necked in death, Virginia.

FROM SEVEN ODES TO SEVEN NATURAL PROCESSES

Ode to Rot

Der gute Herr Gott
said, "Let there be rot,"
and hence bacteria and fungi sprang
into existence to dissolve the knot
of carbohydrates photosynthesis
achieves in plants, in living plants.
Forget the parasitic smuts,
the rusts, the scabs, the blights, the wilts, the spots,
the mildews and aspergillosis—
the fungi gone amok,
attacking living tissue,
another instance, did Nature need another,
of predatory heartlessness.
Pure rot
is not
but benign; without it, how
would the forest digest its fallen timber,
the woodchuck corpse
vanish to leave behind a poem?
Dead matter else would hold the elements in thrall—
nitrogen, phosphorus, gallium
forever locked into the slot
where once they chemically triggered
the lion's eye, the lily's relaxing leaf.

All sparks dispersed
to that bad memory wherein the dream of life
fails of recall, let rot
proclaim its revolution:
the microscopic hyphae sink
their fangs of enzyme into the rosy peach
and turn its blush a yielding brown,
a mud of melting glucose:
once-staunch committees of chemicals now vote
to join the invading union,
the former monarch and constitution routed

by the riot of rhizoids,
the thalloid consensus.

The world, reshuffled, rolls to renewed fullness;
the oranges forgot
in the refrigerator "produce" drawer
turn green and oblate
and altogether other than edible,
yet loom as planets of bliss to the ants at the dump.
The banana peel tossed from the Volvo
blackens and rises as roadside chicory.
Bodies loathsome with their maggotry of ghosts resolve
to earth and air,
their fire spent and water there
as a minister must be, to pronounce the words.
All process is reprocessing;
give thanks for gradual ceaseless rot
gnawing gross Creation fine,
the lightning-forged organic conspiracy's
merciful counterplot.

Ode to Growth

Like an awl-tip breaking ice
the green shoot cleaves the gray spring air.
The young boy finds his school-pants cuffs
too high above his shoes when fall returns.
The pencilled marks on the bathroom doorframe climb.
The cells rereplicate,
somatotropin
comes bubbling down the bloodstream, a busybody
with instructions for the fingernails,
another set for the epiderm,
a third for the budding mammae,
all hot from the hypothalamus
and admitting of no editing,
lest dwarves result, or cretins, or neoplasms.

In spineless crustaceans
the machinery of molting is controlled
by phasing signals from nervous ganglia
located, often, in the eyestalks, where these exist.
In plants
a family of auxins,
shuttling up and down,
inhibit or encourage cell elongation
as eventual shapeliness demands,
and veto lateral budding while apical growth proceeds,
and even determine abscission—
the falling of leaves.
For death and surrender
are part of growth's package.

"It's just the eye's way of growing,"
my ophthalmologist euphemizes
of the lens's slow stiffening
and irreversible presbyopia.
Skin goes keratinous,
the epiphyses of the long bones unite with the shaft,
and "linear growth comes to an end."
Comes to an end!
Our aging's a mystery, as is our sleep:
the protein codes, transactions more elaborate
than the accounts of a thousand dummy trusts,
have their smuggling secrets still.

The meanwhile, let us die
rejoicing,
as around us uncountable husks
are split and shed by the jungle push of green
and the swell of fresh bone
echoes the engendering tumescence.
Time's line being a one-way street,
we must walk the tight rope or fly.
Growth is life's lockstep;
we shall never again sit next to Peggy Lutz

in third grade, her breasts
a mere glint on the curve of her tomboy vigor
and our whiskery doom
within us of less dimension than a freckle.

Ode to Healing

A scab
is a beautiful thing—a coin
the body has minted, with an invisible motto:
In God We Trust.
Our body loves us,
and, even while the spirit drifts dreaming,
works at mending the damage that we do.
That heedless Ahab, the conscious mind,
drives our thin-skinned hull onto the shoals;
a million brilliant microscopic engineers below
shore up the wound with platelets,
lay down the hardening threads of fibrin,
send in the lymphocytes, and supervise
those cheery swabs, the macrophages, in their clean-up.
Break a bone, and fibroblasts
knit tight the blastema in days.
Catch a cold, and the fervid armies
swarm to blanket our discomfort in sleep.
For all these centuries of fairy tales poor men
butchered each other in the name of cure,
not knowing an iota of what the mute brute body knew.

Logically, benevolence surrounds us.
In fire or ice, we would not be born.
Soft tissue bespeaks a soft world.
Yet, can it have been malevolence
that taught the skinned knuckle to heal
or set the white scar on my daughter's glossy temple?
Besieged, we are supplied,
from caustic saliva down,

with armaments against the hordes,
"the slings and arrows," "the thousand natural shocks."

Not quite benevolence.
Not quite its opposite.
A perfectionism, it would almost seem,
stuck with matter's recalcitrance,
as, in the realm of our behavior, with
the paradox of freedom.
Well, can we add a cubit to our height
or heal ourselves by taking conscious thought?
The spirit sits as a bird singing
high in a grove of hollow trees whose red sap rises
saturated with advice.
To the child as he scuffles up an existence
out of pebbles and twigs
and finds that even paper cuts, and games can hurt,
the small assemblage of a scab
is like the slow days' blurring of a deep disgrace,
the sinking of a scolding into time.
Time heals: not so;
time is the context of forgetting and of remedy
as aseptic phlegms
lave the scorched membranes,
the capillaries and insulted nerves.
Close your eyes, knowing
that healing is a work of darkness,
that darkness is a gown of healing,
that the vessel of our tremulous venture is lifted
by tides we do not control.
Faith is health's requisite:
we have this fact in lieu
of better proof of *le bon Dieu.*

MUNICH

Here Hitler had his first success, disguised
as failure. No plaque commemorates the *Putsch*
or marks the hall where Chamberlain begged peace.
Broad avenues and gazing monuments
devoted to the Wittelsbachs and feats
of old Bavarian arms command perspectives
askew with frolicsome façades that mask
riots of silvered rococo within.

The bombs fell lightly here; a burnt-out church
alone eludes the grasp of restoration.
The beer halls smile, the traffic purrs, the young
look innocent as sleeping animals.
The vegetables are stacked like giant jewels
in markets far removed from earth and blood.

A PEAR LIKE A POTATO

Was it worms, having once bitten
and then wilted away, or some canker
known only to nurserymen? Whatever the reason, the pear
fresh-plucked from my tree where it leans and struggles
in the garden's dappled corner
is a heavy dwarf-head whose faceless face
puckers and frowns around a multitude of old problems,
its furrowed brow and evil squint and pursy mouth
and pinched-in reptilian ear rescrambling,
feature for feature, as I rotate
this weight in my hand, this
friendly knot of fruit-flesh, this
pear like a potato.

It wanted to grow, and did. It
had a shape in mind, and if that shape
in transit was waylaid by scars, by cells that turned
too obdurate to join in with the general swelling
and stalled instead, leaving dents between bulges
like quilt-buttons, well, it kept on going
and rests here in my hand ripe and ready,
sun-warmed, to be eaten.

Not bad. The teeth must pick their spots,
between the potato-eyes. Sun's warmth
mingles sweetly with mine. Our brains
are like this, no doubt, having swelled
in spite of traumas, of languages
we never learned, of grudges never set aside but grown around,
like parasites that died but forever snapped
the rhythm whereby cell links up to cell
to make up beauty's smoothness. Plato's
was a manner of speaking, perfection's
an idea there at the start, that
the body and soul make a run at

*

and, falling short, fill the world instead
with the lopsided jumble that is: the congregation
of the failed yet not uncheerful,
like this poor pear
that never would do at the supermarket,
bubble-wrapped with symmetrical brothers, but
has given me a snack,
a nibble here and there, on my own land,
here in the sun of a somewhat cloudy morning.

AIRPORT

Palace of unreality, where the place
we have just been to fades from the mind—shrinking
to some scribbled accounts, postcards unmailed,
and faces held dear, let go, and now sinking
like coins in clouded, forgetful water—
and the place we are heading toward hangs forestalled
in the stretched and colorless corridors,
on the travelling belts, and with the false-

smiling announcements that melt in mid-air:
to think, this may be our last reality.
Dim alcoves hold bars well-patronized but where
there is not that seethe of mating, each he and she
focused instead on a single survival.
To pass through, without panic: that is all.

OXFORD, THIRTY YEARS AFTER

The emperors' heads around the Sheldonian
have been replaced: grotesque great noggins
Roman in style, modern in mocking manner,
sculptured lips ajar, drill-holed eyes a-goggle.
Well, it kept some Council artist busy
for a year or two, and off the dole.
The Fifties heads were rotten, eyeless, blackened,
the limestone leprous yet imperial—

the mind supplied what had been lost to time.
Elsewhere, little change; the long-revered
resists where the new succumbs. Our cafeteria
is gone, but cast-iron gates and hallowed archways
still say *keep out*, *not yours*, *all mine* beneath
old England's sky of hurrying gray stones.

KLIMT AND SCHIELE CONFRONT THE CUNT

That women in their marble glory still
had pubic hair so startled Ruskin he
turned impotent, and had to be divorced.
The nineteenth century, for all its love
of facts, preferred its female hair to stream,
like emanations of divinity,
a ghostly river, solely from the head.

Vienna, though, was looking lower. Freud
sat giving ear above that mystic couch
where golden heads, and brown, materialized
to spill their minds' secretions; meanwhile, Klimt
and Schiele pencilled pussies blackly on
their nudes and even limned the labia
that frame the blameless hole men seek and dread.

For stylish Gustav Klimt, whose early work
shows much of Edvard Munch's hysteria—
such staring, snake-haired, toxic femmes fatales!—
the pubic patch (once lightly called,
by young Adele Astaire, the "Ace of Spades")
plays hide-and-seek beyond a bent-down head
or tucked between the buttocks, just a curl.

For Egon Schiele, born much closer to
la fin de siècle (*fin* is feminine,
men will observe), the pencil gouges deeper,
and something close to famine dulls the eyes
while fingers seek the masturbator's groove.
The flesh is gaunt and splotchy but alive,
and appetite torments its toothless mouth.

RETURNING NATIVE

What can you say about Pennsylvania
in regard to New England except that
it is slightly less cold, and less rocky,
or rather that the rocks are different?
Redder, and gritty, and piled up here and there,
whether as glacial moraine or collapsed springhouse
is not easy to tell, so quickly
are human efforts bundled back into nature.

In fall, the trees turn yellower—
hard maple, hickory, and oak
give way to tulip poplar, black walnut,
and locust. The woods are overgrown
with wild-grape vines, and with greenbrier
spreading its low net of anxious small claws.
In warm November, the mulching forest floor
smells like a rotting animal.

A genial pulpiness, in short: the sky
is soft with haze and paper-gray
even as the sun shines, and the rain
falls soft on the shoulders of farmers
while the children keep on playing,
their heads of hair beaded like spider webs.
A deep-dyed blur softens the bleak cities
whose people palaver in prolonged vowels.

There is a secret here, some death-defying joke
the eyes, the knuckles, the bellies imply—
a suet of consolation fetched straight
from the slaughterhouse and hung out
for chickadees to peck in the lee of the spruce,
where the husks of sunflower seeds
and the peace-signs of bird feet crowd
the snow that barely masks the still-green grass.

*

I knew that secret once, and have forgotten.
The death-defying secret—it rises
toward me like a dog's gaze, loving
but bewildered. When winter sits cold and black
on Boston's granite hills, in Philly,
slumped between its two polluted rivers,
warmth's shadow leans close to the wall
and gets the cement to deliver a kiss.

SQUIRRELS MATING

In fits and starts around
and around the hickory's
adhesive trunk, they
chase one another—or
so it seems, though the male
must be doing the chasing
and the female the fleeing,
without ever seeming
to flee very far, or to be
quite out of it. Back in it,
rather. Around and
around the trunk in a
furry flurry, they stop
and start, up and down,
a double helix halted when,
deadpan, he mounts her, and
she, expressionless
in kind but palpably
alert and sensitive and strong,
supports their two linked weights
by clinging with her two
front feet, as frail as burrs,
to bark. The male, his tail
erect and quivering with faith,
hangs on to only her,
their four bright beady eyes
turned outward to the world.
Sun shines. Leaves shake. The slow
world turns. The moment passes,
the primal freeze-frame. Then,
as skittery as ever, they—
our innocent, unsatisfied
Sciuridae—resume
their chase in fits and starts.

SAILS ON ALL SAINTS' DAY

One does not expect to see them, out there,
so late, on a sea so blue, beneath this sky
whose faint clouds seem to be remembering
yesterday's skywriting. True, the sails are few,
and the wind they are tilting in is a mystery.
A freighter stands out in Massachusetts Bay
like a small gray tab on a giant folder marked
FILE IN MEMORY. This calm at winter's edge.

More toward the foreground, trees, their blushing done,
look burnt, and the frost-defying roses
incongruous. The summer's last flies find
my warm white corner, where a leaning mop,
set out to dry, plays the hypotenuse
to its own slim shadow, mast-straight and blue.

TULSA

Not Oral Roberts' city of heavenly glitz
(as are most dreams come true, in dreadful taste)
nor the Gilcrease Museum's thirty thousand
arrowheads and countless canvases
of melting cowboys in pathetic-prairie pink,
but vacant lots impressed me most: downtown
a wilderness of parking space and brave
renewal schemes—the least false note, pawn shops.

Oil money like a flash flood came and went;
one skyscraper was snapped off like a stick
when the big ebb hit. Now the Arkansas
pokes muddily along, and a rusty train
fills all that hollow downtown with a blast
the Cherokee street people blink away.

IN MEMORIAM FELIS FELIS

The Pussycat on Causeway Street is closed.
Vacant the poster cases that proclaimed
RED HOT, ADULT, and UNINHIBITED.
Dusty and chained the glass doors opening
into the small slant lobby where a black
bored woman took your fiver and a turn-
stile yielded as if a subway lay beyond.
Dark, dark at noon the theatre had been,
its inky seats as silent as the tomb.
Your fear was sitting on a sleeping bum.
The screen would be ablaze with private parts,
and hollow breathless voices spelled a plot
whose only point was reached recurrently,
at bright pink junctures flecked with pubic hair.
The actors' voices smacked of youth, L.A.,
and nervousness subdued. The girls' bare forms,
most pallid in their bulges, testified
to mornings sunning on the beach before
the dawn of these exploitive afternoons.
Tans are an enemy of sex; the boys
were brown and fair and could not get it up
beneath the camera's cool lascivious eye,
though lapped and coaxed enough to rouse the dead.
The bits of film where actors, clothed, advanced
the feeble plot were touching—fumbled, mouthed
like Christmas pageants, Mary just a girl.
You knew you soon would see her stripped; in this
she was, this L.A. starlet, like a wife.

Your eyes grew accustomed; the flickering
picked out still shapes—men's heads, some bowed, some raised
and awash in the carnal, jerky glow,
but all well-spaced, no two adjacent, dumb
ruminants grazing their turf in dreamland.
Young males, their cheeks exuberant with acne,
in Boston for a toot; old Chinamen;
commuters with an hour before the train
dragged them home to suburban spice in frocks;

and alcoholic angels copulating
could not distract from stupor and their thirst:
as in an ill-attended church, our heads
in scatteration showed a stubborn faith,
a sly propensity to praise. What a thing
a woman is! No end to her sufferance,
her spirit of coöperation, or
her elasticity and rosy grace!
The tints of every rose from black to white,
from purple proud in her cleft to surface cream,
became her beauty; mercy swallowed shame.
Succumb to the wrecker's ball, closed Pussycat,
like a hooker jeering at her arrest.
There's more indecency than meets the eye.
Bald light will break into you like a drug
that kills the good bacteria with the bad;
a thousand furtive lusts will throng the sun
and form a cloud as fertile as the id.

ENEMIES OF A HOUSE

Dry rot intruding where the wood is wet;
   hot sun that shrinks roof shingles so they leak
and bakes pane-putty into crumbs; the pet
   retriever at the frail screen door; the meek
small mice who find their way between the walls
   and gnaw improvements to their nests; mildew
in the cellar; at the attic window, squalls;
   loosening mortar; desiccated glue;
ice backup over eaves; wood gutters full
   of leaves each fall and catkins every spring;
      salt air, whose soft persistent breath
turns iron red, brass brown, and copper dull;
   voracious ivy; frost heaves; splintering;
      carpenter ants; adultery; drink; death.

CONDO MOON

When plans were announced to tear down
the garages behind the main street and put up
twelve units of condos, there was a protest
the board of aldermen narrowly overrode.
Now, as I stroll from behind the "convenience store,"
the moon like a tasteful round billboard
hangs wheat-field yellow over the far fake turret
of the condos' massed neo-shingle-style bulk.

The moon makes no protest. It rolls what it sees
into the scene it illumines, and lends its old weight—
afloat and paper-thin and scarred with *maria*—
to what men have thrown up as once it beamed benign
on Crusader castles, fern swamps becoming coal,
and the black ocean when no microbe marred it.

THE BEAUTIFUL BOWEL MOVEMENT

Though most of them aren't much to write about—
mere squibs and nubs, like half-smoked pale cigars,
the tint and stink recalling Tuesday's meal,
the texture loose and soon dissolved—this one,
struck off in solitude one afternoon
(that prairie stretch before the late light fails)
with no distinct sensation, sweet or pained,
of special inspiration or release,
was yet a masterpiece: a flawless coil,
unbroken, in the bowl, as if a potter
who worked in this most frail, least grateful clay
had set himself to shape a topaz vase.
O spiral perfection, not seashell nor
stardust, how can I keep you? With this poem.

TO A BOX TURTLE

Size of a small skull, and like a skull segmented,
of pentagons healed and varnished to form a dome,
you almost went unnoticed in the meadow,
among its tall grasses and serrated strawberry leaves
your mottle of amber and umber effective camouflage.

You were making your way through grave distances,
your forefeet just barely extended and as dainty as dried
coelacanth fins, as miniature sea-fans, your black nails
decadent like a Chinese empress's, and your head
a triangular snake-head, eyes ringed with dull gold.

I pick you up. Your imperious head withdraws.
Your bottom plate, hinged once, presents a *No*
with its courteous waxed surface, a marquetry
of inlaid squares, fine-grained and tinted
tobacco-brown and the yellow of a pipe smoker's teeth.

What are you thinking, thus sealed inside yourself?
My hand must have a smell, a killer's warmth.
It holds you upside down, aloft, undignified,
your leathery person amazed in the floating dark.
How much pure fear can your wrinkled brain contain?

I put you down. Your tentative, stalk-bending walk
resumes. The manifold jewel of you melts into grass.
Power mowers have been cruel to your race, and creatures
less ornate and unlikely have long gone extinct;
but nature's tumults pool to form a giant peace.

FALL

October 1989

The undertaker, who was with the local minister
and the neighboring farmer when they broke in,
made a wry face and hinted at damage
too dreadful to be viewed—"a cut in the eye,
a lot of blood." I took his kindly offer not
to view the corpse but looked, back in the house,
in the kitchen corner where she fell, head crushing
the paper bag she used for trash. She was eighty-five.
Her heart had floated to a stop and she dropped
without lifting a hand or averting her face.

What corner or edge might have given the gash?
I saw none, then saw her glasses, a circle and half
of plastic frames, the one lens popped
and skipped a foot away amid the dust.
I picked it all up, and the little wool hat
(it was getting to be fall) she wore for warmth,
with a spot of dried blood on the blue threads.
She seemed so very small in these her remnants.
"Oh, Mama," I said aloud, though I never called
her "Mama," "I didn't take very good care of you."

PERFECTION WASTED

And another regrettable thing about death
is the ceasing of your own brand of magic,
which took a whole life to develop and market—
the quips, the witticisms, the slant
adjusted to a few, those loved ones nearest
the lip of the stage, their soft faces blanched
in the footlight glow, their laughter close to tears,
their tears confused with their diamond earrings,
their warm pooled breath in and out with your heartbeat,
their response and your performance twinned.
The jokes over the phone. The memories packed
in the rapid-access file. The whole act.
Who will do it again? That's it: no one;
imitators and descendants aren't the same.

WORKING OUTDOORS IN WINTER

It can be done. The seal of frost
imposed upon the windows can
be broken, and a depth of air revealed.
Trees follow one another, one by one—
birch, beech, white oak, a hickory or ash—
and make a space to move in, space
like that inside your clothes,
which can be warmed.
                                        The poison ivy dormant,
mosquitoes dead, and leaves' green suffocation
lifted, you wield the clipper, swing the ax
in an atmosphere of freedom earned, of nature
as calligraphy, transparent to the will.
You overheat, at last, and seem to wound
the virgin quiet as a glowing poker
wounds the water it is plunged into.

To build a fire in winter's heart!
Now, *there* is self-assertion, gathering
the heap of brush, the castoff branches,
the kindling wood and match, and tools
to keep the orange pet in bounds, its roar
and snap and snarl and singing hiss all yours,
Der Feuermeister.
                              The blue smoke soils
blue sky, an ascent of sparks describes an S
baroque as the sound holes in a violin,
and a bed of frozen earth is fried,
with all its sleeping worms. The cold day sinks
to its ruddy ash of dusk while you recall
in bone and vein what tough machines
men are, their burning gristle built to push
against the zero waiting all around.

GRANITE

New England doesn't kid around;
it wears its bones outside.
Quartz-freckled, time-rumpled granite—
your tombstone everywhere.

At night I wake and warily gaze
at outcroppings on my lawn.
These moonlit humpbacks, do they sleep
or do their blanched surfaces sense my eyes?

By day, you can see how earth
engenders itself over aeons—
pine needles silt in, and tender weeds
take hold in the cracks, then wild roses

and hairy-stemmed sumacs find enough
for a footing, and oak rootlets,
and out of the mesh comes a mulch, a soil—
trapped particles breed trapped life.

There is no way not to die,
can it be? What do these stones
coldly know? Or is moonlight warm,
and the granite a pledge

to which consciousness clings?
Better rock than the mud
of a meaningless mercy, such as men
would devise. This outcrop

is a wide gray glow the night has grown.
I think with awe of the man
who will gaze down upon it, awake,
when I'm blinder than stone.

NOVEMBER

The light the sun withdraws the leaves replace
   in falling, sweeping clean the clouded sky.
This brightness shocks the window like a face.

Our eyes contract to hold the sudden space
   of barrenness—bare branches, blue, up high.
The light the sun withdrew has been replaced.

The tiny muscles of the iris taste
   past time—old falls, slant light—recalling why
this brightness shocks the window like a face.

To children, years are each a separate case,
   enormous, full of presents and surprise:
the light the sun withdraws the leaves replace.

For grown-ups, reminiscence scores the days
   with traces veteran nerve-ends recognize
when brightness shocks the window like a face.

November, we know you—the grudging grace
   of clarity you grant the clouded eye.
The light the sun withdraws the leaves replace
with brightness at the window like a face.

FLY

What have we done this winter to deserve
this plague of giant flies? They breed in the house,
being born to batter and buzz at the glass
of windows where sunshine shows a world of snow.

Stupid out of season, they are easy to swat,
and some can't seem to fly, but run across
the kitchen linoleum in a comical hurry,
more like a frantic man than you would think.

Stupid myself one noon, I watched one primp
head-down on a sunstruck kitchen wall.
He rubbed his face on his rotating head
with forelegs finer than a pencil line;

a cleansing seemed in progress, bit by bit.
He held each wing out stiff, its rainbow shadow
projected down the wall diagonally,
and scrubbed the membranes with a fussy leg.

All creatures groom, but who would figure that
a fly, which thrives on dirt, could be so nice?
His head and legs were like a watchworks ticking,
but spaced by intervals of what seemed thought.

His interlocking parts' complexity
was photocopied by his lengthened shadow,
a sharp mechanical drawing sunshine drew:
each twitch, each quick caress of mouth-parts,

each hinge of animate anatomy.
Up from a maggot had arisen this tower
of microcosmic beams, their third dimension
craned outward to contain a fourth, called life.

*

So how can I crush construction so rare?
A bomber flattens cities but cannot see
the child in the map, the network of girders.
Swat not, not I at the moment, all eye.

BINDWEED

Intelligence does help, sometimes;
the bindweed doesn't know
when it begins to climb a wand of grass
that this is no tree and will shortly bend
its flourishing dependent back to earth.

But bindweed has a trick: self-
stiffening, entwining two- or three-ply,
to boost itself up, into the lilac.

Without much forethought it manages
to imitate the lilac leaves and lose
itself to all but the avidest clippers.

To spy it out, to clip near the root
and unwind the climbing tight spiral
with a motion the reverse of its own
feels like treachery—death to a plotter
whose intelligence mirrors ours, twist for twist.

JULY

Deep pools of shade beneath dense maples,
the dapples as delicious as lemon drops—
textures of childhood, and its many flavors!
The gratefulness of cool, the bottles of
sarsaparilla and iodine-red cream soda
schooled like fish, on their sides,
in the watery ice of the zinc-lined cooler
in the shade of the cherry trees
planted by the town baseball diamond,
where only grown-ups cared what the score was
and the mailman took his ups with a grunt
that made the crowd in its shirtsleeves laugh.
The sun kindled freckles like a match
touching straw, and beneath a tree
a quality reigned like the sound of a gong,
solemn and sticky and calm. Then the grass
bared the hurry of ants, and each blade
bent to some weight, some faint godly tread
we could not see. The dapples
were not holes in the shade but like pies,
bulging up, and air tasted of water,
and water of metal, and metal of what
would never come—real change, removal
from this island of stagnant summer,
the end of sarsaparilla and its hint
of licorice taste, of sassafras twig,
of things we chewed with the cunning of Indians,
to whom all trees had souls, the maples no more
like birches than clouds are like waterfalls.
The dying grass smelled especially sweet
where sneakers had packed it flat,
or out of the way, in the playground corner,
where the sun had forgot to stop shining.
This was the apogee, July, a month
like the piece of a dome where it flattens
and reflects in a smear high above us,
the ant-children busy and lazy below.

TO A DEAD FLAME

Dear X, you wouldn't believe how curious
my eyebrows have become—jagged gray wands
have intermixed with the reddish-brown, and poke
up toward the sun and down into my eyes.
It hurts, a self-caress that brings tears
and blurred vision. Aches and pains! The other day
my neck was so stiff I couldn't turn my head
to parallel-park. Another man
would have trusted his mirrors, but not I;
I had the illusion something might interpose
between reality and its reflection, as happened with us.

The aging smell, X—a rank small breeze wafts upward
when I shed my underwear. My potency,
which you would smilingly complain about,
has become as furtive as an early mammal.
My hair shows white in photographs, although
the barber's clippings still hold some brown.
At times I catch myself making that loose mouth
old people make, as if one's teeth don't fit,
without being false. *You're well out of it*—
I tell you this mentally, while shaving
or putting myself to bed, but it's a lie.

The world is still wonderful. Wisps of mist
were floating off your old hill yesterday,
the hill where you lived, in sight of the course
where I played (badly) in a Senior Men's
Four-Ball in the rain, each green a mirage.
I thought of us, abed atop that hill,
and of how I would race down through your woods
to my car, and back to my life, my heart
enormous with what I newly knew—
the color of you naked, the milk of your sighs—
through leaves washed to the glisten of fresh wounds.

*

What desperate youthful fools we were, afraid
of not getting our share, our prize in the race,
like jostling marathoners starting out,
clumsy but pulsingly full of blood.
You dropped out, but we all drop out, it seems.
You never met my jealous present wife;
she hates this poem. The living have it hard,
not living only in the mind, but in
the receding flesh. Old men must be allowed
their private murmuring, a prayer wheel
set spinning to confuse and stay the sun.

ELDERLY SEX

Life's buried treasure's buried deeper still:
a cough, a draft, a wrinkle in the bed
distract the search, as precarious as
a safecracker's trembling touch on the dial.
We are walking a slack tight wire, we
are engaged in unlikely acrobatics,
we are less frightened of the tiger than
of the possibility the cage is empty.

Nature used to do more—paroxysms
of blood and muscle, the momentous machine
set instantly in place, the dark a-swim,
and lubrication's thousand jewels poured forth
by lapfuls where, with dry precision, now
attentive irritation yields one pearl.

ACADEMY

The shuffle up the stairs betrays our age:
sunk to polite senility our fire
and tense perfectionism, our curious rage
to excel, to exceed, to climb still higher.
Our battles were fought elsewhere; here, this peace
betrays and cheats us with a tame reward—
a klieg-lit stage and numbered chairs, an ease
of prize and praise that sets sheath to the sword.

The naked models, the Village gin, the wife
whose hot tears sped the novel to its end,
the radio that leaked distracting life
into the symphony's cerebral blend.
A struggle it was, and a dream; we wake
to bright bald honors. Tell us our mistake.

NOT CANCELLED YET

Some honorary day
if I play my remaining cards right
I might be a postage stamp
but I won't be there to lick me
and licking was what I liked,
in tasty anticipation of
the long dark slither out of the mailbox,
from box to pouch to hand
to bag to box to slot to hand
again: that box is best
whose lid slams open as well as shut,
admitting a parcel of daylight,
the green top of a tree,
and a flickering of fingers, letting go.

DOWNTIME

Waiting for Tom, the boy who can fix my computer if anybody can,
I observe how the minutes, emptied of content,
ooze past like transparent microörganisms,
in magnification's slow motion. I have time
at last to consider my life, this its stubby stale end—
whither, and wherefore, and who says?
But I fail to. I look out the window again.
A wisp from the woods announces that my neighbor is burning brush.
Wind tugs the rising plume this way and that,
a signifier that doesn't know its mind.
My desktop is cluttered, but what
can be discarded utterly with certainty
of its not coming back to haunt us from the kingdom of the lost?
My wife no longer acts like a mistress,
but surely I am too frail to seek a mistress;
passé the pink salmon's slick effortful flipping
up the icy, carbonated cataracts.
Is there anything to write about but human sadness?
Even if there were, I couldn't write it today.
My neighbor's smoke has stopped rising; his fire, too, is down.

IN THE CEMETERY HIGH ABOVE SHILLINGTON

We fifth-grade boys would thread tricolor strips
of crêpe paper through our bikes' staggered spokes,
and spiral-wrap the handlebars, and ride
in Shillington's Memorial Day Parade.
With many a halt, while gold-roped drums kept up
their thrilling, hiccupping tattoo, we moved—
the Legion bands, the shuffling vets—along
Lancaster Avenue, then up New Holland
past Mr. Shverha's movie house, where war
was cheerful weekly fare, and death more sweet
than anything we learned in Sunday school,
to this bright static ground above the town.
A granite mausoleum stated LOEB.
The nasal pieties rang hollowly
above the sunstruck flags and sharp-edged stones;
we dimly listened, kidded and horsed around
there on the grit and grass, and pedalled home.

Have fifty years gone by since last I turned
into these unlocked gates? In rented car,
on idle impulse, briefly home, if "home"
is understood as where one was a child,
I glide into this long-forgotten space
carved from a flank of bosky Cedar Top,
my tires gently crackling as I park.
The town's drab rooftops fan out from my feet.
The month is June; the seasonal flags
and potted memorial flowers still are fresh.
Sole visitor, by knocking with my eyes
on graven, polished portals set in rows
I find here what the live town lacks, some friends—
some people I once knew. Many the time,
from well within our hedged-in yard, or out
our cloudy front-room windows, did I spy
with awe and wonderment the pure-white head
of Pappy Shilling, whose father had been
the town's creator and Ur-citizen,
the subdivider of a primal farm.

So short that even a child could sense willed pride,
Pap looked too old to be a son. His cane
was ebony black; a chain of Lutheran badges
hung twittering from his blue lapel; his bangs
of cornsilk bobbed in keen-eyed childhood's glare.
He seemed a doll-man living up the street,
his house more grand than ours, and more hedged-in.
Named Howard M., he died, his granite claims,
in 1943. Eleven years
we shared on Philadelphia Avenue,
lives overlapped like trapeze artists' wrists.

Some strides away, the headstone titled BECKER
remembers OREVILLE, dead in '57.
Within my witness, Parkinson's disease
had watered his gaze to a groggy stare,
yet in his prime he was a nobleman
whose name had taken on the might of place:
Becker of Becker's Garage, its gas and grease
and oil-black floor and multitude of tools,
its blanching hiss of hot acetylene
and shelves of numbered parts and sliding doors
that rumbled overhead in tune with casters
that slid supine mechanics back and forth
like jacks of spades in a magician's pack.
My father, after school or playing hookey
for half an hour, would sit and puff a Lucky
Strike by the grease pit's edge, his run-down heels
up on the pipe guardrail in cocky style.
He owed his teaching job to Oreville, who
had swayed the school board toward the son-in-law
of Katie (Kramer) Hoyer, his wife's aunt.
ELSIE, not dead till 1970,
was one of three (like Graces) Kachel sisters,
a Kachel having wed another Kramer.
She crammed her house, next door to the Garage,
with bric-a-brac on whatnots; to a child
her knickknacks breathed of pious opulence,

as did her thickly laden Yuletide tree.
Her Kramer blood bid Elsie to be kind
to all of us, the Updikes and the Hoyers;
my humpbacked, countrified grandma was thus
our link to local aristocracy.
Without the Beckers, our newcomers' place
in Shillington would have been small indeed.

Pink polished stone adorned with mating birds
announces COLDREN—FATHER ELLWOOD E.,
SON ELLWOOD H. (his life's parenthesis
opened and closed in 1922),
and MOTHER STELLA M. Can this mute rock
be Woody Coldren, who with booming voice
and flapping arms would lead us town tots through
a storm of carols Christmas morning from
the movie house's curtained, shallow stage?
He hid the sorrow of a soon-dead child
behind a plethora of public works—
of heading up the Sunday school, of being
the borough's burgess, of bringing Noël home
full-throatedly, between a few cartoons
of Disney manufacture and the gift
of a with-almonds nickel Hershey bar
straight from Mr. Shverha's Jewish hand.
Many in this community could sing—
the German knack of *Lieder*, probably—
and I, a croaky dunce at song, was yet
enlisted snugly under Woody's boom,
within the *civitas* he cheerled on.

Here neighbors, LUTZes, lie. Across the street,
at 112 Philadelphia Avenue,
the two of them would sit upon their porch
and gaze toward our less-fertile domicile.
Proud GORDON ran the local ice plant, source
of gutter water babbling like a brook
and of slow-melting blocks our icebox held,

while MAMIE did her duty as the source
of, yes, eleven children. Herman, Floyd,
Ted, Dick, and Russell formed a five-star flag
the Reading *Eagle* featured in its news.
Five sons they sent to war, and all came back.
Their stone is near-eclipsed by potted homage
—geraniums, petunias, marigolds—
a portion of their scattered spawn has paid.
Ample in form, sly in mien, this mother
of warriors was one of the neighborhood's
watchers, who made my life feel witnessed—small
but visible in her complacent view.

But who sleeps here, nearby? Another LUTZ,
a LEWIS R., born 1928.
Can this be Looie, long-legged Looie Lutz,
who'd race down through our yard to save three steps
en route to Shillington High, where he excelled
at basketball and track, until football
bestowed a blow that left his head off-tune?
My father always called football a crime
for still-maturing bodies, and cited Looie
to prove his point. What took him to the grave
so early, speedy Looie, just four years
my senior? He became a postman, whom
I met on Philadelphia Avenue
one soft fall day, across the street from where
he used to dash, trespassingly,
along our walk, down through our arbored grapes
behung with buzzing Japanese-beetle traps,
on past our birdbath, ruffling my mother's feathers,
and through the lower hedge into the alley.
As I recall, my elders muttered in
their kitchen consultations but did not
pollute the neighborhood with a complaint,
and now that Looie's raced to join the dead
with his unbroken stride, I'm just as glad.

*

Few shade trees here afford the shelter for
a gloomy thought; I search the sun-baked rows
of TOTHEROs and MATZes, OLINGERs
and MILLERs, for one potent name of old,
and find it—HEMMIG, CHARLES J., known as Jack,
whose dates of '93 to '89
add up to near a century. He was
my father's boss, the lord of S.H.S.,
the supervising principal. He read
Ecclesiastes to assembly each
first day of school—"a time to cast away
stones, and a time to gather stones together."
His big head with its timid, thin-lipped smile
seemed to be melting to one side; he had
an oozy unpredictability.
He would appear within my father's class
and send my insecure progenitor
into paroxysms of incompetence.
The man had Roman hands, the senior girls
reported, and like Jupiter could be
ubiquitous, descending as a swan
in Mohnton or, in Grille, a shower of gold.
A stentor of the local charms, a genius
of local politics, he nonetheless
approved my going to Harvard, far away,
and reassured my parents that the leap
was not too daring, too Promethean.

Never shall I lie here, in trimmed green silence,
among the earners of this resting-place,
who underneath the patterned ground extend
the Shillingtonian ethos, the mild
belief that Earth's safe center has been found
beneath the heights of Cedar Top, Slate Hill,
and elevations cold ambition climbs.
I am your son; your mile-square grid of brick—
the little terraces, the long back yards—
contains my dream of order, here transposed

to an eternal scale. The flags will fade
and tatter, the flowers will turn to litter
before next May will wheel around again
its formal protest against the forgetting
that lets the living live. We were too young,
we boys on bikes, to hide the giddy bliss
of floating over people freed from need,
a field of buried guardians who bar
the pathway back with sharp-edged swords of stone.

61 AND SOME

How many more, I must ask myself,
such perfect ends of Augusts will I witness?—
the schoolgirls giggling in their months-old tans,

reviving school gossip as they hang on the curbs,
as brown as maple seeds, the strip of curbside grass
sun-parched in the ragged shade beneath the maple

that in its globular cloud of green cumulus
holds now an arc, a bulge of rouge,
held up to the bored blue sky like a cheek to kiss.

AMERICANA

(Poem Begun on Thursday, October 14, 1993, at O'Hare Airport, Terminal 1, Concourse B, around Six O'Clock P.M.)

Gray within and gray without: the dusk
is rolling west, a tidal wave of shadow
that gently drowns Chicago. Overhead,
the gray steel arches of this much-admired
architectural essay in public space
blend with gray sky and distill a double
sense of semi-enclosure, of concealment
in a universal open that includes:
the airfield with its pomp of taxiing
fresh-landed smooth-nosed behemoths;
the feeder highway sloping to an underpass
not far beyond a gray-ribbed wall of glass;
the taillights blazing ruby as autos brake
and fume with passion in the evening jam;
the silvery Midwestern sky, its height
implying an oceanic stretch of grain
whose port is this diffuse metropolis.
Without, translucent clouds; within, mute hordes
of travelling strangers, numinous, their brisk
estrangement here a mode of social grace.
No two touching as they interweave
and dodge in the silent interior dusk
beneath the mock cathedral arches, each
soul intent, each ticketed, each rapt
with a narrow vision, these persons throng
my heart with a rustle of love, of joy
that I am among them, where night and day,
mingling, make a third thing, a betweentimes
of ecstatic layover and suspension.

Women in gray jackets matching those
of men, above their taut gray skirts, and blacks
striding enlivened by the dignity
of destination, and children unafraid
of being lifted up in aluminum arms;

brightly colored pools of candy bars; the men's
room prim beside the equal-access WOMEN;
briefcases floating in a leather flock;
announcements twanging in the transfixed air
where cloudy faces merge and part again,
a cumulus of ghosts advancing, stern
yet innocent of everything but time,
advancing through me to their set departures,
through walls of gray, as nearby taillights burn
more furious in their piecemeal, choked descent.
Another fine transparency of film
is added to the evening's shining weight
of lovely nothingness, among machines.

This poem—in ballpoint, on a torn-off scrap
of airline magazine—got lost, along
with several boarding passes, ticket stubs,
and airline napkins. Now it seeks me out
here in New Jersey, on November 5th,
a Friday, in a Fairfield Radisson
that overlooks an empty parking lot.
At dusk, the painted stripes devoid of cars
are like unplayed piano keys aligned
within the drizzle that is lacquering
the Garden State. Beyond: Route 46;
an unknown mall; a stream of traffic glowing
white in the one direction, red in the other.
This poem again, its kiss of ecstasy
among waste spaces, airy corridors
to somewhere else, where all men long to be.
I strain my eyes, as neon starts to tell
its buzzing, shoddy tale; across the stream
of traffic hangs a weathered sign that spells
AMERICAN WAY MALL. The hotel room—
the shapes of luxury in cut-rate textures—
offers nothing superfluous, not even
a self-important so-called "scratchpad" near
the telephone, where travellers might write

how strangely thrilled they were to pass this way,
the American way, where beauty is left
to make it on its own, with no directives
from kings or cultural commissars on high.
It emerges, it seeps forth, stunning us
with its grand erosions of the self;
its grit of atomisms and fleet inklings
can carve a canyon or function as a clock
that wakes to tick one single tick a day.

The poem evaporates, a second time
is lost, and then a third, in your reading
here and now, which turn to there and then
as dampness overtakes, quick molecule
by molecule, the glowing moment
when God's gray fire flickers on the edge
of the field of vision like a worm of flame
that struggles to consume a printed page.

A WOUND POSTHUMOUSLY INFLICTED

A stapled brown book-envelope
containing the bound galleys of
a posthumous book by a man
who once was my Harvard roommate
pricked me in the finger, painfully,
between the first and second joints.

Kit was prickly even then, in 1950,
slouching across the black-painted
floorboards of Hollis Hall, holding
out his hand in sheepish welcome. We
were mated, our troth plighted
by the deans' psychic accountants.

Both "interested in writing," both white,
both Gentile, though he had been raised
by progressive Midwestern parents
as an atheist and I by Something-fearing
Pennsylvanians as a Lutheran,
an old wooden cross in my luggage.

An unexpressible friction chafed
during our silent hours as,
both scared products of public schools,
our desks a stride apart, we strove
to make the grade, our gooseneck lamps
glaring into the assigned pages.

Love, of a kind. He cleaned up the mess
when I returned blind drunk, throwing up,
from my *Lampoon* initiation.
In beds side by side, we improvised
musical comedies and, bored at last,
suppressed the rustle of our masturbation.

He used to worry about losing his hair,
yet kept a head fuller than mine.
When last we met, after a cooling-off

of thirty years or more, he was sweet,
and looked at me as if I had amused him
all along, while we lived our lives—

our ponytailed, bluestockinged wives,
plucked fresh from the college stacks;
our quartets of children, engendered
as if by quota in some square world
of Eisenhower normalcy;
our careers and affairs, if any.

He had become a learned grump, and I
a literary Mr. Sunshine.
I resisted reading his books, and he
could not have found much time for mine.
Yet still, Kit, to reach out and stab me
this way, from beyond the grave!—

your first overtly hostile act,
not counting the sulks you could throw.
My naïve faith exasperated you.
I played bad golf all yesterday,
my finger sore and hurting just where
the grip is supposed to rest.

VENETIAN CANDY

How long will our bewildered heirs
marooned in possessions not theirs
puzzle at disposing of these three
cunning feignings of hard candy in glass—
the striped little pillowlike mock-sweets,
the flared end-twists as of transparent paper?

No clue will be attached, no trace
of the sunny day of their purchase,
at a glittering shop a few doors
up from Harry's Bar, a disappointing place
for all its testaments from Hemingway.
The Grand Canal was also aglitter
while the lesser canals lay in the shade
like snakes, flicking wet tongues
and gliding to green rendezvous.

The immaculate salesgirl, in her aloof
Italian succulence, sized us up,
a middle-aged American couple,
as unserious shoppers who,
still half jet-lagged, would cling to their lire
in the face of any enchanted vase
or ethereal wineglass that might shatter
in the luggage going home.

Yet we wanted something, something small. . . .
This? No . . . How much is ten thousand? Dizzy,
at last we decided. She wrapped
the three glass candies, the cheapest
items in the shop, with a showy care
worthy of crown jewels—tissue,
tape, and tissue again sprang up
beneath her blood-red fingernails,
plus a jack-in-the-box-shaped paper bag
adorned with harlequin lozenges, sad
though she surely was, on her feet waiting

all day for a wild rich Arab, a compulsive Japanese.
Grazie, signor . . . grazie, signora . . . ciao.

Nor will our thing-weary heirs decipher
the little repair, the reattached triangle
of glass from the paper-imitating end-twist,
its mending a labor of love in the cellar,
by winter light, by the man of the house,
mixing transparent epoxy and rigging
a clever small clamp as if to keep
intact the time that we, alive,
had spent in the feathery bed
at the Europa e Regina.

TWO CUNTS IN PARIS

Although stone nudes are commonplace—some crammed
two to a column, supple caryatids,
and others mooning in the Tuileries—
the part that makes them women is the last
revelation allowed to art; the male
equipment, less concealable, is seen
since ancient times: a triune thingumbob.

Courbet's oil, *L'Origine du monde,* was owned
by Madame Jacques Lacan and through some tax
shenanigans became the Musée d'Orsay's.
Go see it there. Beneath the pubic bush—
a matted Rorschach blot—between blanched thighs
of a fat and bridal docility,
a curved and rosy closure says, *"Ici!"*

We sense a voyeur's boast. The *Ding an sich,*
the thing as such, a centimeter long
as sculpted, *en terre cuite,* in fine detail
of labia and perineum, exists
in La Musée des Arts Décoratifs,
by Clodion, *dit* Claude Michel. A girl
quite young and naked, with perfected limbs

and bundled, banded hair, uplifts her legs
to hold upon her ankles a tousled dog
yapping in an excitement never calmed:
the sculptor caught in suavely molded clay
this canine agitation and the girl's,
the dark slits of her smile and half-shut eyes
one with the eyelike slit she lets us view.

*

Called *La Gimblette* (“ring-biscuit”—a low pun?),
this piece of the eternal feminine,
a doll of femaleness whose vulval facts
are set in place with a watchmaker’s care,
provides a measure of how short art falls
of a Creator’s providence, which gives
His creatures, all, the homely means to spawn.

ONE TOUGH KERATOSIS

My hands have had their fun, and now must suffer.
A wealth of sun, especially on the right,
un-golf-gloved hand, pays dividends of damage:
white horny spots, pre-cancerous, that grow
until the squinting dermatologist
hits back by spraying liquid nitrogen,
which stings like a persistent, icy bee.

One spot especially fascinated me—
a trapezoidal chip of cells gone wrong
between my wrist and thumb, in vexing view
whenever I wrote or gestured. Blasted, it
sat up on a red blister, then a scab.
How hideous! Obsessing helplessly,
I couldn't quell my wishing it away,

and yet it clung, a staring strange bull's-eye
both part of me and not, like consciousness
or an immortal, ugly soul. I touched
it morning, noon, and night, a talisman
of human imperfection and self-hate.
The dermatologist had botched his job,
I thought; death only would unmar me. Then

it fell off in a New York taxicab.
I brushed it lightly, settling back, and felt
a kind of tiny birth-pang near my thumb.
Release! I picked up from the seat this flesh
no longer me—so small and dry and meek
I wondered how the thing had held, so long
and fiercely, my attention. Fighting down

an urge to slip it in my jacket pocket
to save among my other souvenirs,
or else to pop it in my mouth and give

those cells another chance, I dropped it to
the dirty taxi floor, to join Manhattan's
unfathomable trafficking of dust.
A tidy rosy trace has still to heal.

THE WITNESSES

From Anne Frank's house in Amsterdam
(steep hidden stairs, and some unfurnished rooms,
and, in a case, a child's small, tartan-covered
diary) to the synagogue in Prague
where, in a ceremonial hall once used
for cleaning Jewish dead for burial,
drawings by children held at Terezín
are on display, the horror speaks in terms
of interrupted innocence. The dead are dead;
the guards, administrators, torturers,
and railwaymen have gone to hell for good,
and underfoot there lies atrocity
so vast that every forest voice was stilled
but these, of hatchlings wakening at night.

ICARUS

O.K., you are sitting in an airplane and
the person in the seat next to you is a sweaty, swarthy gentleman of Middle Eastern origin
whose carry-on luggage consists of a bulky black briefcase he stashes,
in compliance with airline regulations,
underneath the seat ahead.
He keeps looking at his watch and closing his eyes in prayer,
resting his profusely dank forehead against the seatback ahead of him,
just above the black briefcase,
which if you listen through the droning of the engines seems to be ticking, ticking
softly, softer than your heartbeat in your ears.

Who wants to have all their careful packing—the travellers' checks, the folded underwear—
end as floating sea-wrack five miles below,
drifting in a rainbow scum of jet fuel,
and their docile hopes of a plastic-wrapped meal
dashed in a concussion whiter than the sun?

I say to my companion, "Smooth flight so far."
"So far."
"That's quite a briefcase you've got there."
He shrugs and says, "It contains my life's work."
"And what is it, exactly, that you do?"
"You could say I am a lobbyist."

He does not want to talk.
He wants to keep praying.
His hands, with their silky beige backs and their nails cut close like a technician's,
tremble and jump in handling the plastic glass of Sprite when it comes with its exploding bubbles.

Ah, but one gets swept up
in the airport throng, all those workaday faces,
faintly pampered and spoiled in the boomer style,
and those elders dressed like children for flying
in hi-tech sneakers and polychrome catsuits,
and those gum-chewing attendants taking tickets

while keeping up a running flirtation with a uniformed bystander, a stoic blond
pilot—
all so normal, who could resist
this vault into the impossible?

Your sweat has slowly dried. Your praying neighbor
has fallen asleep, emitting an odor of cardamom.
His briefcase seems to have deflated.
Perhaps not this time, then.
But the possibility of impossibility will keep drawing us back
to this scrape against the numbed sky,
to this sleek sheathed tangle of color-coded wires, these million rivets, this wing
like a frozen lake at your elbow.

UPON BECOMING A SENIOR CITIZEN

March 18, 1997

The day, another grudging chill installment
of slow spring in New England, moves my mind
to Pennsylvania, the growing boy
curled above the comics amid four elders.
Early, before I scamper off to school
to hear my peers sing out the usual song
to me and Harlan Boyer, my birthday twin,
my grandfather, a sly and toothless smile
tucked under his ashen mustache, slides forward
in soft black squeaking high-top buttoned shoes
to hold out in his onionskin-dry hand
a single, folded dollar bill. Why should
this creased and meagre gift outdo in magnitude
all gifts received since then? His wallet, thin
and polished, lived a secret life. He stirred
the fire in the cellar awake each dawn
and each spring turned the vegetable garden
chocolate shovelful by shovelful.
Older even than I am now, he capped
with a country wheeze the most reflective of
his spoken sentences. A thumbnail held
near enough to the eye blots out the sun;
we hug those first years and their guardians
so close to spite the years that took away
the days of trolley cars, coal furnaces,
leaf fires, knickers, and love from above.

A RESCUE

Today I wrote some words that will see print.
Maybe they will last "forever," in that
someone will read them, their ink making
a light scratch on his mind, or hers.
I think back with greater satisfaction
upon a yellow bird—a goldfinch?—
that had flown into the garden shed
and could not get out,
battering its wings on the deceptive light
of the dusty, warped-shut window.

Without much reflection, for once, I stepped
to where its panicked heart
was making commotion, the flared wings drumming,
and with clumsy soft hands
pinned it against a pane,
held loosely cupped
this agitated essence of the air,
and through the open door released it,
like a self-flung ball,
to all that lovely perishing outdoors.

JACOPO PONTORMO

Pontormo, hailed by Michelangelo
when just nineteen—"he will exalt
this art unto the heavens, if he lives
and perseveres"—did persevere. The dukes
and monks imposed commissions. His masterpiece,
The Deposition in Santa Felicità,
scorns gravity; Christ's body seems to rise
through clouds of blue-and-pink bewilderment.

The rumpled robes are empty as balloons,
the stares evasive as a Kewpie doll's,
the feet attached to earth by just one toe.
He worked alone and dressed in rags. His brain
"strayed into vagaries." Strenuous forms
he seized were robbed of weight; the Renaissance,
its gilded, weeping, papal piety,
became the painted shell of dead belief.

JESUS AND ELVIS

Twenty years after the death, St. Paul
was sending the first of his epistles,
and bits of myth or faithful memory—
multitudes fed on scraps, the dead small girl
told *"Talitha, cumi"*—were self-assembling
as proto-Gospels. Twenty years since pills
and chiliburgers did another in,
they gather at Graceland, the simple believers,

the turnpike pilgrims from the sere Midwest,
mother and daughter bleached to look alike,
Marys and Lazaruses, you and me,
brains riddled with song, with hand-tinted visions
of a lovely young man, reckless and cool
as a lily. He lives. We live. He lives.

REPLACING SASH CORDS

It's easier to screw than to unscrew;
the heads have generally been painted in,
and the slots need to be chipped open. Then
the side strips pop free in a shower of flakes,
revealing the stained unpainted doors, secured
by two rust-whittled nails, to the chambers
where wait the sash weights, somber and inert.

The frayed cord snapped; a sash weight dropped one night
when no one listened. Here it rests, on end,
the simulacrum of a phallus, long,
blunt-ended, heavy, rough, its heaviness
its raison d'être, so rust and ugliness
don't matter, nor the dreadful loneliness
of being hung for decades in the dark.

Stiffened and dried by time, the knots
still yield to prying fingers. They are not
all alike; there were a number of hands;
most settled for a pair of half-hitches,
but some displayed a jaunty sailor's skill
and love of line, looped back and proudly cinched.
Dead handymen and householders less deft

come forth from these their upright wooden tombs
with a gesture, a swirl of rope before
they let the sash weight drop and, knocking, swing
back to its dark mute duty, its presence
known only in the grateful way a window,
counterbalanced, lightly rises to
admit the hum and eager air of day.

THE HEDGE

In boyhood's verdure, as if underwater,
my mother and her ancient father struggle
with a rusty brown eel, one on each end—
our iron hedge-trimmer, turned by a crank,
its two toothed levels gnashing back and forth
like the contention between parent and child.

How pink my mother's face would get! How grim
the gray of Grandpa's mustache and fedora,
its sweated brim twin to his soaked suspenders.
The hedge enclosed the wide front yard, its corners
right-angled caves where octopi might lurk
in depths of privet only a child would see.

Pride, pride of property, kept us going.
The hedge, like a leafy solid by Magritte,
had round raised intervals to reinforce
an illusion of fortress strength. In fact
we were a feeble crew; the Depression
had left us mere shadows behind our hedge.

Frail Grandma ran up a flag on Memorial Day,
on a thin tin pole. The infrequent guests
and the mailman came up a red-brick walk.
The impregnable hedge, a dry-eyed visit
some decades later told me, has vanished—
the yard, so small, barer than an old rug.

SONG OF MYSELF

What devil in me likes the early dark?
My wife inveighs against Daylight Saving
but I accept that what was light-filled six
is now a twilit five,
and noon has the feel of one,
and one of an hour as far advanced as two.

The time is growing short, the shadows say,
till dinner's healing candlelight. Why
am I lately so slow to heal?
A cut at the corner of my lips—
the dentist's steely fingers reopened it.

A finger I painfully smashed, right on the cuticle,
when a fast-sliding filing-cabinet drawer
closed with my mind momentarily elsewhere—
weeks and weeks later, I watch
the squarish purple two-tone wound
move slowly out on the injured nail.
Will I live to clip it off?

Our bodies love us more than our minds do.

The slit wrists of suicides heal,
the psychotic's banged skull,
the slashes of drink-mad knife-fighters—
gray welts in the elastic black skin.
My white skin is horny with sun damage,
yet still it encloses the bone.

At night, I lie down to sleep
in a sort of cosmic sourness, the sweat of my mind.
The death-dealing quasars at the void's far rim
come visit me to share their nullity—
splendid in their case,
ignominious in mine.

*

God, that dwindled residue.

My mind mocks itself as I strive to pray,
to squeeze from a dried-up creed
enough anaesthetizing balm
to enroll me among sleep's tranced citizenry,
who know no void nor common sense.

Sleep is a strange city. Even
the terror there, the embarrassments—
being naked in a supermarket, and smeared with shit—
have a healing, purgative effect.
When they lift, we are grateful
for reality, terminal though it be.

Each morning I reclaim,
reluctantly at first,
the threads of yesterday,
pulling my arms from beneath the covers
to marvel once more at my hands,
five-petalled shadows in the bedroom gloom.
I take up my body and walk.

Tomorrow is the shortest day of the year,
but by some cosmic trick, some wobble
in the earth's working-out of its spin,
the sunset has already been arriving
later each afternoon—a bed
of red coals that flares up in the woods,
yet does them no damage.

The two-tone purple spot
on my fingernail is moving out,
but slowly, so slowly,
and the keratin behind it
doesn't look smooth and healthy, as it did.
All wounds are inflicted for good.

*

My two new tooth implants—
are they fusing to the bone?
They sleep beneath my sutured gums
like chiggers of titanium.
The dentist's drill kept slipping,
with a gnashing my skull bones amplified;
he sweated in his intensity of skill.

My face, draped in antiseptic paper and painted,
was deep in anaesthesia, so my mind
could take a detached stance as he struggled;
but then his drill went deeper
than the anaesthesia had gone,
discovering a nerve not asleep.

I grunted in alarm, in savage protest.

He had found beneath
the skin of civilized life
the unanswerable outrage, the hot coal.
When the sliding drawer smashed my cuticle
the pain was worse even than the time
the Bucklins' yellow Labrador leaped at the fence
and fell back with my finger in his teeth.

Those scars are still there,
pale fang trails,
fading and among the lesser
of the cellular atrocities
that mar the backs of my hands.

These are always in my sight, like two open pages
of a detestable yet gripping book—
unevenly scorched, pricked up in points
as of Braille spelling an unheeded warning,

my life outdoors distilled
to these dry nubs
of microscopic breakage.

Countless hours . . . except the molecular clock
was keeping count. Tires whose treads
are worn down to the underlying threads
can be replaced with new.
So, less easily, hips and teeth. But skin
there is no trading in.

Used bodies—who wants them
save Death, the great rag-and-bone man?
We are hostages trussed in our wrinkles,
blindfolded with cataracts,
handcuffed to our painful spines.

Where else to go, who else to be,
here at this intersection of borrowed hours,
this dark wobble on the distant pivot,
blurring away our earned flaws, turning our hides
as smooth as the glossy pelt of night
in the forest fed by its own shed leaves?

The shame of time . . . yet what force else
will stir the galaxies, rotate the cells,
arrange each day's fresh, healing coat
until the last, annulling one?

My skin and I have shared a life
with something else, that rides and sees.

TO A SKYLARK

Upon the lonely links, above the abundant rough,
you mount with ragged, insistent song
heavenward, far heavenward, then fall,
by staged descent, seeking a level of air
that sets your spirit off to best advantage—
a most congenial perch in breezy emptiness,
from which you sink, aflutter, to a lower,
there trembling like a leaf on thread-thin stem.

Some spot on earth holds you, some phantom nest
that roots your flighty, singing vertical.
Like cries of a crowd of children unseen,
your lone song floods the grass-floored void. I am rapt,
lifted from my earthbound plight—my life, my game—
and freed by empathy with sheer blithe being.

RELIGIOUS CONSOLATION

One size fits all. The shape or coloration
of the god or high heaven matters less
than that there is one, somehow, somewhere, hearing
the hasty prayer and chalking up the mite
the widow brings to the temple. A child
alone with horrid verities cries out
for there to be a limit, a warm wall
whose stones give back an answer, however faint.

Strange, the extravagance of it—who needs
those eighteen-armed black Kalis, those musty saints
whose bones and bleeding wounds appall good taste,
those joss sticks, houris, gilded Buddhas, books
Moroni etched in tedious detail?
We do; we need more worlds. This one will fail.

SAYING GOODBYE TO VERY YOUNG CHILDREN

They will not be the same next time. The sayings
so cute, just slightly off, will be corrected.
Their eyes will be more skeptical, plugged in
the more securely to the worldly buzz
of television, alphabet, and street talk,
culture polluting their gazes' dawn blue.
It makes you see at last the value of
those boring aunts and neighbors (their smells
of summer sweat and cigarettes, their faces
like shapes of sky between shade-giving leaves)
who knew you from the start, when you were zero,
cooing their nothings before you could be bored
or knew a name, not even your own, or how
this world brave with hellos turns all goodbye.

A SOUND HEARD EARLY ON THE MORNING OF CHRIST'S NATIVITY

The thump of the newspaper on the porch
on Christmas Day, in the dark before dawn
yet after Santa Claus has left his gifts:
the real world reawakens; some poor devil,
ill-paid to tear himself from bed and face
the starless cold, the Godforsaken gloom,
and start his car, and at the depot pack
his bundle in the seat beside his own
and launch himself upon his route, the news
affording itself no holiday, not even
this anniversary of Jesus' birth,
when angels, shepherds, oxen, Mary, all
surrendered sleep to the divine design,
has brought to us glad tidings, and we stir.

BOCA GRANDE SUNSET

Big Mouth, FL, where all the billionaires
are pushing out the millionaires—so goes
the local joke. Sand is a dollar a grain.
Still, the sunset comes free, and clutter-free,
done with a circle and straight line. The Gulf
has given up its Caribbean tint
already and unrolls metallic breakers
in gilded flight from the sinking sore orb,

which, touching the horizon, changes form
like an invading molecule sucked oblong
at a membrane's verge. It turns barn-shape,
broad red; is half a disc, and then a tent
trembling; then less, and is doused. A gull flaps home
through bloodied skies. Event succeeds event.

REALITY

Displacing our plausible dream piece by piece—
the sun beneath the shade, the bedside lamp,
the saliva-moistened pillow—it asserts its rights
gently, certain of its ancient ground.
It knows it must prevail, though we turn
away into the blankets again, and drink
deep for minutes more of that alternative
where the unreal prevails and heals our sores.

Reality like a mild but inflexible mother
stands waiting in the wallpaper and the view
worn thin in the windows by blind seeing.
The bed will not make itself, the teeth will rot
unbrushed, the bladder's ache cries for release,
the world prates its promises and stale laws.

CHICORY

Show me a piece of land that God forgot—
a strip between an unused sidewalk, say,
and a bulldozed lot, rich in broken glass—
and there, July on, will be chicory,

its leggy hollow stems staggering skyward,
its leaves rough-hairy and lanceolate,
like pointed shoes too cheap for elves to wear,
its button-blooms the tenderest mauve-blue.

How good of it to risk the roadside fumes,
the oil-soaked heat reflected from asphalt,
and wretched earth dun-colored like cement,
too packed for any other seed to probe.

It sends a deep taproot (delicious, boiled),
is relished by all livestock, lends its leaves
to salads and cooked greens, but will not thrive
in cultivated soil: it must be free.

RAINBOW

Short storms make the best rainbows—
twenty minutes of inky wet, and then,
on the rinsed atmosphere's curved edge,
struck by the reëmergent sun
in oversize, glorious coinage,
mint-fresh from infra-violet to ultra-red,
ethereal and rooted in the sea
seen through it, dyeing a bell-buoy green,

it has appeared. And when it fades, today,
it leaves behind on the bay's flat glaze
a strange confetti of itself, bright dots
of pure, rekindled color, neon-clear.
What on earth? Lobster-pot markers,
speckling the brine with polychrome.

SHINTO

Who living would not love red, the *torii* gates
lacquered like fingernails, and how the shrines
just wait, beneath the cedars, with their stalls
peddling embroidered charms, for what to happen?
For you to make a wish: for a believer,
however weak, to step up and clap his hands,
twice, sharply, saying to the spirits, "Here
I am, look at me, my head bowed, and listen."

There is/are *kami* everywhere, but here
and there more than elsewhere. It has to do
with Nature. The emperor, a living god,
pleasures the sun-goddess with rice and wine:
hush-hush. For him, the *kamikaze* died.
The altars hold no Buddha, just a muddle,
a chair of sorts, a mirror, dull and distant,
a minimum to pray to. Who wants more?

DECEMBER SUN

December sun is often in your eyes,
springing a foliage of lashy rays
and irritating dazzle, to replace
the foliage now stripped from all the trees.
The planet rolls and tilts beneath our feet;
the tilt obscurely works to clip the day
a minute shorter; coldness infiltrates
the web of sticky seconds and we freeze.

The year! We're chained to it as to a wheel
that breaks us, but so slowly we don't feel
a thing except at sunset, or sunrise,
when shallow angles form a kind of knife
that slices through the friendly fat of days
and bares the clock that ticks until we die.

BIG BARD

O what a lark it must have been to be
Shakespeare—to face no copyediting,
to never blot a line, to spell a word
the way you wished, or wisht, just anyhow,
without a spinsterish consistency,
so future editors could spend a year
and quarts of ink deciphering what you
or swinish printers botched in a second's lapse;

to be a happy hack, and take the plots
that Burbage thought would set him nicely off,
and make them rippling spills of golden spieling,
with buffoon bits worked in for Kempe and Armin;
to rip off homosexual sonnets, yet spend
a Stratford weekend now and then with Anne;
to be adored by crown and groundlings both;
to be profound, immortal, smooth, and quick;

to be (to quote Ben Jonson) "honest," with
"an open, and free nature" plus "brave notions,
and gentle expressions" on top of "an
excellent *Phantsie*" and "that facility,
that sometime . . . should be stop'd"; to be the pet
of Harold Bloom and Northrop Frye; to sell
like mad in paperback, and outlive Marlowe,
and die scarce able to scratch your name—pure lark!

WACO

The local Hilton, situated near
the Roeblings' old suspension bridge (a trial
attempt, it's said, for their Brooklyn masterpiece,
though built for cattle drives across the Brazos),
contains a bar where four great TV screens
befuddle breakfast eaters with a feast
of twitching imagery, the news gone mad.

Ten miles away, the Branch Davidians'
outmoded news is weathering beneath
a high gray sky; small signs stuck here and there
as on an amateurish battlefield
explain, as best they can, the school bus buried,
the compound bulldozed flat, and, still intact,
the dead messiah's battered motorcycle.

The faithful who survived (some did, and own
this land) are not in view. Instead, a yellow,
youthful mongrel cur, without a collar,
starved for affection yet with a taste for it,
whimpers, leaps, and licks our hands, abject
and wagging; the will to believe lives on
amid these miles of weeds and sorghum fields.

TOOLS

Tell me, how do the manufacturers of tools
turn a profit? I have used the same clawed hammer
for forty years. The screwdriver misted with rust
once slipped into my young hand, a new householder's.
Obliviously, tools wait to be used: the pliers,
notched mouth agape like a cartoon shark's; the wrench
with its jaws on a screw; the plane still sharp enough
to take its fragrant, curling bite; the brace and bit
still fit to chew a hole in pine like a patient thought;
the tape rule, its inches unaltered though I have shrunk;
the carpenter's angle, still absolutely right though I
have strayed; the wooden bubble level from my father's
meagre horde. Their stubborn shapes pervade the cellar,
enduring with a thrift that shames our wastrel lives.

STOLEN

Please go on being yourself.
—*from my last letter from William Maxwell, July 28, 2000*

What is it like, to be a stolen painting—
to be Rembrandt's *Storm on the Sea of Galilee*
or *The Concert* by Vermeer, both burglarized,
along with *Chez Tortoni* by Manet,
and some Degases, from the Isabella Stewart
Gardner Museum, in Boston, twelve years ago?

Think of how bored they get, stacked
in the warehouse somewhere, say in Mattapan,
gazing at the back of the butcher paper
they are wrapped in, instead of at
the rapt glad faces of those who love art.

Only criminals know where they are.
The gloom of criminality enshrouds them.
Why have we been stolen? they ask themselves.
Who has benefitted? Or do they hang
admired in some sheikh's sandy palace,
or the vault of a mad Manila tycoon?

In their captivity, they may dream of rescue
but cannot cry for help. Their paint
is inert and crackles, their linen friable.
They have one stratagem, the same old one:
to be themselves, on and on.

The boat tilts frozen on the storm's wild wave.
The concert has halted between two notes.
An interregnum, sufficiently extended,
becomes an absence. When wise
and kindly men die, who will restore
disappeared excellence to its throne?

EVENING CONCERT, SAINTE-CHAPELLE

The celebrated windows flamed with light
directly pouring north across the Seine;
we rustled into place. Then violins
vaunting Vivaldi's strident strength, then Brahms,
seemed to suck with their passionate sweetness,
bit by bit, the vigor from the red,
the blazing blue, so that the listening eye
saw suddenly the thick black lines, in shapes
of shield and cross and strut and brace, that held
the holy glowing fantasy together.
The music surged; the glow became a milk,
a whisper to the eye, a glimmer ebbed
until our beating hearts, our violins
were cased in thin but solid sheets of lead.

ELEGY FOR A REAL GOLFER

Payne Stewart, I remember courtesy of TV
how you nearly burst in boyish joy
when you sank that uphill fifteen-footer—
not a simple putt, and you charged it—
to win the 1999 Open at Pinehurst.

You were a butternut-smooth blond Southerner
and the plus fours made you look cocky,
and the smile with a sideways tug to it,
but you didn't deserve to die that unreal way,
snuffed out by failed oxygen in a private jet

that rode the automatic pilot up and down
like a blind man doing the breast stroke
at forty thousand feet, for hours,
with its asphyxiated cargo, till the fuel ran out
and a charred hole marred South Dakota soil.

This end, so end-of-the-twentieth-century,
would not stick in my mind as a luminous loss
had I not, while marshalling at the '99
Ryder Cup matches, on the seventh fairway
at The Country Club in Brookline, watched

the parade of golfers marching down the fourth,
pausing in foursomes to hit their second shots.
In all that parade, Payne Stewart, you
had the silkiest swing, so silky
its aftermath shimmered in air: dragonfly wings.

BIRD CAUGHT IN MY DEER NETTING

The hedge must have seemed as ever,
seeds and yew berries secreted beneath,
small edible matter only a bird's eye could see,
mixed with the brown of shed needles and earth—
a safe, quiet cave such as nature affords the meek,
entered low, on foot, the feathered head
alert to what it sought, bright eyes darting
everywhere but above, where net had been laid.

Then, at some moment mercifully unwitnessed,
an attempt to rise higher, to fly,
met by an all but invisible limit, beating wings
pinioned, ground instinct denied. The panicky
thrashing and flutter, in daylight and air,
their freedom impossibly close, all about!

How many starved hours of struggle resumed
in fits of life's irritation did it take
to seal and sew shut the berry-bright eyes
and untie the tiny wild knot of a heart?
I cannot know, discovering this wad
of junco-fluff, weightless and wordless
in its corner of netting deer cannot chew through
nor gravity-defying bird bones break.

SAGUAROS

They look battered and friction-worn, although
they never go
anywhere, but stand for a century or two
as if playing statue
out in the humorless sun
and the cold-faced moon. Their fun
is sombre fun, clumsy fun, without a word.
The hummingbird
and the cactus wren
inhabit their thorny mockery of men,
each miming gesture
slightly unprecedented in Nature.
Their melancholy individuality
spells death to me;
their skeletons outlast their flesh, as with us,
  and as in many a howling congregation
  their arms lift up in surrender or supplication.
Mute mobs of them throng the desert dusk.

OUTLIVING ONE'S FATHER

I could feel, above me,
the hunger in his stride, the fear
that hurled him along an edge
where toothaches, low pay, discipline
problems in the classroom were shadows
of an all-dissolving chaos.

At his side, his shorter only offshoot,
I both sheltered and cowered. He was fallible
but doughty, even cocky as he drove
disintegrating pre-war cars down Reading's
rattling streets, past coal yards,
candy stores, and dives
whose lurid half-glimpsed doings amused
his Presbyterian soul, bred of a Trenton manse.

The Middle Atlantic region was the humid hell
where he showed me how to go unscorched
by neon and glaring sidewalks. He
had been there before, my guide. Now where
can I shelter, how can I hide,
how match his stride
through years he never endured?

DEATH OF A COMPUTER

Eight years of stories, novels, book reviews—
the daily grind. *Someday it's going to crash,*
I was assured, and so, an insecure
computer dilettante, I bought a new
and tucked the old in an odd room, where, when
I plugged it in again, it took old disks
and turned them into final printed versions,
dark marks on paper safer than electrons
after all. The mechanism seemed
not to resent semi-retirement.

Today, it died; I think it died. First sign:
a ghostly square imposed itself upon
the text, like "inappropriate" behavior
that casts a shadow on a gathering but
can be ignored. Then, at the next command,
black stripes appeared, bejewelled with tiny bits
of shattered icons; it performed much as
a one-time lawyer in a senile fit
springs up to address the jury with
the trademark flourishes and folksy candor.

The pointing arrow then began to trail
black pixels like a painter's dripping brush.
Split second to split second, the monitor
believed itself to still be making sense,
while stripes and streaks and sudden twists transformed
my tapped advice into a rapid havoc;
embarrassed by such bright and hopeful garble,
I in a spurt of mercy shut it down.
May I, too, have a stern and kindly hand
bestow upon my failing circuits peace.

LUCIAN FREUD

(An exhibit in Venice, September 2005)

Yes, the body is a hideous thing,
the feet and genitals especially,
the human face not far behind. Blue veins
make snakes on the backs of hands, and mar
the marbled glassy massiveness of thighs.
Such clotted weight's worth seeing after centuries
(Pygmalion to Canova) of the nude
as spirit's outer form, a white flame: Psyche.

How wonderfully Saint-Gaudens' slim Diana
stands balanced on one foot, in air, moon-cool,
forever! But no, flesh drags us down,
its mottled earth the painter's avid ground,
earth innocently ugly, sound asleep,
poor nakedness, sunk angel, sack of phlegm.

VACATION PLACE

The space grows smaller. The sense of release
has yielded to another, of an end
to possibilities in this small piece
of borrowed territory where we spend
a week or month to cease to be ourselves,
environs lighter than accustomed air,
our bureau drawers less burdened, and the shelves
of paint-free poplar innocently bare.

We heard at first all silence. Voices now,
whose owners we know, pierce the morning; cars
afflict the gravel; starlings make a row;
worn routines creak; hungry for mail, we starve.
Dear flimsy quasi-home, we'll miss your view,
but life is more than viewing; it's to do.

DOO-WOP

Does anyone but me ever wonder
where these old doo-wop stars you see
in purple tuxedos with mauve lapels
on public-television marathons
have been between the distant time when they
recorded their hit (usually only one,
one huge one, that being the nature of doo-wop)
and now, when, bathed in limelight and applause,
the intact group re-sings it, just like then?

They have aged with dignity, these men,
usually black, their gray hairdos still conked,
their up-from-the-choir baby faces lined
with wrinkles now, their spectacles a-glimmer
upon their twinkling eyeballs as they hit
the old falsetto notes and thrum-de-hums,
like needles dropped into a groove, the groove
in which both they and we are young again,
the silent years skipped over.
                                        Who knows
what two-bit gigs and muddled post-midnights
they bided their time in? And when at last
the agitated agent's call came through—
the doo-wop generation old enough
and rich enough by now to woo again,
on worthy telethons this time around,
nostalgia generating pledges—why
was not a weathered man of the quartet
deceased or otherwise impaired? How have
they done it, come out whole the other side,
how did they do it, do it still, still doo?

FRANKIE LAINE

(1913–2007)

The Stephens' Sweet Shop, 1949.
Bald Walt at work, "butterflying" hot dogs—
splitting them lengthwise for the griddle
and serving them up in hamburger buns—
while Boo, his smiling, slightly anxious wife
(a rigid perm and excess, too-bright lipstick),
provides to teen-aged guzzlers at the counter
and in an opium den of wooden booths
their sugary poisons, milkshakes thick as tar
and Coca-Cola conjured from syrup and fizz.

A smog of smoke. The jingle at the back
of pinball being deftly played. And through
the clamorous and hormone-laden haze
your slick voice, nasal yet operatic, sliced
and soared, assuring us of finding our
desire, at our old rendezvous. Today
I read you died, at ninety-three. Your voice
was oil, and we the water it spread on,
forming a rainbow film—our futures as
we felt them, dreamily, back there and then.

BASEBALL

It looks easy from a distance,
easy and lazy, even,
until you stand up to the plate
and see the fastball sailing inside,
an inch from your chin,
or circle in the outfield
straining to get a bead
on a small black dot
a city block or more high,
a dark star that could fall
on your head like a leaden meteor.

The grass, the dirt, the deadly hops
between your feet and overeager glove:
football can be learned,
and basketball finessed, but
there is no hiding from baseball
the fact that some are chosen
and some are not—those whose mitts
feel too left-handed,
who are scared at third base
of the pulled line drive,
and at first base are scared
of the shortstop's wild throw
that stretches you out like a gutted deer.

There is nowhere to hide when the ball's
spotlight swivels your way,
and the chatter around you falls still,
and the mothers on the sidelines,
your own among them, hold their breaths,
and you whiff on a terrible pitch
or in the infield achieve
something with the ball so
ridiculous you blush for years.
It's easy to do. Baseball was

invented in America, where beneath
the good cheer and sly jazz the chance
of failure is everybody's right,
beginning with baseball.

HER COY LOVER SINGS OUT

> When she's in love, she says, "It totally consumes me. I want to be with that person every minute of every day. I want to sleep with him and eat with him and talk with him and breathe the air he breathes."
>
> —*from the* Boston Globe, *about Doris Day*

Doris, ever since 1945,
when I was all of thirteen and you a mere twenty-one,
and "Sentimental Journey" came winging
out of the juke box at the sweet shop,
your voice piercing me like a silver arrow,
I knew you were sexy.

And in 1962, when you
were thirty-eight and I all of thirty
and having a first affair, while you
were co-starring with Cary Grant in *That Touch of Mink*
and enjoying, according to the *Globe,*
Doris's Red-Hot Romp with Mickey Mantle,
I wasn't surprised.

Now in 2008 (did you ever,
think you'd live into such a weird year?),
when you are eighty-four and I am seventy-six,
I still know you're sexy,
and not just in reruns or on old 45 rpms.
Your four inadequate husbands weren't the half of it.

Bob Hope called you Jut-Butt, and your breasts
(Molly Haskell reported)
were as big as Monroe's but swaddled.
Hollywood protected us from you,
the consumed you, what the *Globe* tastefully terms
the "shocking secret life of America's Sweetheart."

*

Still, I'm not quite ready
for you to breathe the air that I breathe.
I huff going upstairs as it is.
Give me space to get over the *idea* of you—
the thrilling silver voice,
the gigantic silver screen. Go
easy on me. *Cara,* let's take our time.

ENDPOINT

March Birthday 2002, and After

Beverly Farms, MA

Mild winter, then a birthday burst of snow.
A faint neuralgia, flitting tooth-root to
knee and shoulder-joint, a vacant head,
too many friendly wishes to parry,
too many cakes. Oh, let the years alone!
They pile up if we manage not to die,
glass dollars in the bank, dry pages on
the shelf. The boy I was no longer smiles

a greeting from the bottom of the well,
blue sky behind him from a story book.
The Philco sings out "Hi-yo" by his sickbed;
he thinks that Mother, Father, mailman, and
the wheezy doctor with his wide black bag
exist for him, and so they do, or did.

*

Wife absent for a day or two, I wake
alone and older, the storm that aged me
distilled to a skin of reminiscent snow,
so thin a blanket blades of grass show through.
Snow makes white shadows, there behind the yews,
dissolving in the sun's slant kiss, and pools
itself across the lawn as if to say,
Give me another hour, then I'll go.

The lawn's begun to green. Beyond the Bay—
where I have watched, these twenty years, dim ships
ply the horizon, feeding oil to Boston,
and blinking lights descend, night after night,
to land unseen at Logan—low land implies
a sprawl of other lives, beneath torn clouds.

*

Raw days, though spring has been declared.
I settle in, to that decade in which,
I'm told, most people die. Then, flying south,
I wonder why houses in their patterned crowds
look white, whatever their earthbound colors,
from the air. Golf courses, nameless rivers.
The naked Connecticut woods hold veins
of madder like the green veins of the sea.

The pilot takes us down Manhattan's spine—
the projects, Riverside cathedral, Midtown
bristling up like some coarse porcupine.
We seem too low, my palms begin to sweat.
The worst can happen, we know it from the news.
Age I must, but die I would rather not.

*

Not yet. Home safe. New England's vernal drought
has taken a hit this week of sleety rain.
Spent harbingers, the snowdrops lie
in drenched, bedraggled clumps, their tired news
becoming weeds. The crocuses drink in
the leaden air and spread their stained-glass cups
to catch the filtered sun clapboards reflect,
and daffodils grow leggy like young girls.

Nature is never bored, and we whose lives
are linearly pinned to these aloof,
self-fascinated cycles can't complain,
though aches and pains and even dreams a-crawl
with wood lice of decay give pause to praise.
Birthday, death-day—what day is not both?

03/18/03

Beverly Farms

Birthday begun in fog, shot through with light—
"eating the snow," they used to say. The *Globe*
this morning adds a name to those I share
the date with: Wilson Pickett, Brad Dourif,
F. W. de Klerk, Vanessa Williams,
my pal George Plimpton, plus Hawaiian statehood.
The name is Queen Latifah, whom I've seen
in several recent movie hits. Sweet smile.

A day so blank, I take a walk, the way
my parents used to do in Sunday's calm.
Through woods, in boots, the snowmelt turning leaves
to soggy mats. A lack of tracks: I am
the first to walk this path this snowbound spring,
an Adam being nibbled like old ice.

*

The winds of war, warm winds in desert dust,
have been unleashed, the fifth war of my life,
not counting the Cold one, and skirmishes.
Protestors dust off Vietnam's gaudy gear
and mount their irreproachable high nags
called Peace, Diplomacy, and Love.
I think that love fuels war like gasoline,
and crying peace curdles the ears of doves.

Yet something is awry, no doubt of it.
Out on the Bay, a strange steel spider crawls
among our islands, glaring bright at night.
Time was when this white house, with its broad view,
wore blackout shades and watched the iron sea
for submarines. A child then now is old.

*

My parents seemed to sail ahead of me
like ships receding to destinations where
I'd be forgotten. "Wait up!" I wailed,
those Sunday walks a faint pretaste of death.
Today, I tread with care the icy path
and climb the beachside boulders well aware
of how a slip, a misjudged step, might crack
my skull and there I'd lie like limp sea-wrack.

The well-lit thing at night, a neighbor claims,
is laying pipe, for natural gas, to Salem.
But under water? It carries a crane
and freezing men we cannot see—poor men,
who serve from bleak necessity campaigns
conceived in cozy offices. Wait up!

Tucson Birthday, 2004

Ocotillo leafs out beside the porch rail—
saw-teeth of green assault the sky's nude blue.
The cactus wrens chirp in the cholla's shade.
Beyond, the tennis players call it quits.
Downtown, miles stretch like melting tar
beneath the car wheels; desert distances
suffuse the asphalt of the many malls
with fuming, SUV-infested haste.

My mother dreamed of Tucson once, when I
was a boy with no desire to move
or leave my father, which was part of the deal.
Now here I am, the very day she bore me.
I thought my birthday, here, would prove unreal,
but time and sun are not so smoothly fooled.

*

Sun damage—the skin does not forget:
Crane Beach, the Caribbean, hoeing shirtless
the Pennsylvania bean-rows. Cells remember
and wrinkle, pucker, draw up in a knot
the doctor's liquid nitrogen attacks.
And yet, the illusion lingers, light is good
as sent down by the sun, that nearby star
that flattens like a fist, and burns to kill.

They come, the retirees, to bake away
their juicy lifetime jobs, their fertile prime's
no longer potent jism. And I, I scratch
this inconclusive ode to age. It feels
immortal, the sun's dark kiss. The prickly pear
has ears like Mickey Mouse, my first love.

*

To copy comic strips, stretched prone
upon the musty carpet—Mickey's ears,
the curl in Donald's bill, the bulbous nose
of Barney Google, Captain Easy's squint—
what bliss! The paper creatures loved me back
by going about their businesses each day,
and in the corner of my eye, my blind
grandfather's black shoes jiggled when he sang.

The West, our better half, has turned obese.
Vast movie houses hold a quiet handful
of senior citizens bemused by shows
of closely shaved, inane obscenity.
At city limits, numb saguaros hail
with lifted arms the guzzling sunset rush.

The Author Observes His Birthday, 2005

A life poured into words—apparent waste
intended to preserve the thing consumed.
For who, in that unthinkable future
when I am dead, will read? The printed page
was just a half-millennium's brief wonder,
Erasmus's and Luther's Gutenberg-
perfected means of propagating truth,
or lies, screw-pressed one folio at a time.

A world long dulled by plagues and plainsong warmed
to metal's kiss, the cunning kerns and serifs,
the Gothic spears and rounded Roman forms,
the creamy margins smartly justified,
the woodcuts showing naked Mother Eve:
a rage to read possessed the peasantry.

*

The church was right; the Bible freed
spelled trouble. Literate Protestants waged war,
and smashed the Lady Chapels all to Hell,
new-style. No Pope, no priests, no Purgatory—
instead, clear windows and the pilgrim soul,
that self which tribal ways suppressed, and whose
articulation asked a world of books.

A small-town Lutheran tot, I fell in love
with comic strips, Benday, and talk balloons.
The daily paper brought us headlined war
and labor strife; I passed them by en route
to the funnies section, where no one died
or even, saving Chic Young's Blondie, aged.

*

My harried father told me, "Dog eat dog."
I opted for a bloodless universe
of inked imaginings. My mother's books
from college—Shakespeare and Sir Walter Scott,
Lane Cooper, Sinclair Lewis, H. G. Wells—
made peaceful patterns with their faded spines.
I didn't open them, unleashing dogs
too real for me, but sniffed their gentle smell

of paper, glue, and cloth. My many dreams
of future puissance—as a baseball star,
test pilot, private eye, cartoonist, or
as Errol Flynn or Fred Astaire—did not
include a hope to be the hidden hand
and mind behind some musty, clothbound maze.

*

But, then, to see my halt words strut in type!
To see *The Poorhouse Fair* in galley proofs
and taste the candy jacket Harry Ford
cooked up for me! And then to have my spines
line up upon the shelf, one more each year,
however out of kilter ran my life!
I drank up women's tears and spat them out
as 10-point Janson, Roman and *ital.*

When Blanche and Alfred took me out to lunch
he sent the wine right back. *How swell,* I thought.
Bill Maxwell's treat was Japanese; we sat
cross-legged on the floor and ate fish raw,
like gulls. In suit and tie, an author proved
to be, like "fuck" in print, respectable.

*

Back then, my children, in those simpler years
before all firms were owned by other firms,
the checks would come imprinted with a dog,
a bounding Borzoi, or the profile of
a snooty figment, Eustace Tilley. He
was like a god to me, the guardian
of excellence; he weighed my mailed-in words
and paid a grand or so for tales he liked.

A thousand dollars then meant we could eat
for months. A poem might buy a pair of shoes.
My life, my life with children, was a sluice
that channelled running water to my pan;
by tilting it, and swirling lightly, I
at end of day might find a fleck of gold.

*

A writer, stony-hearted as he seems,
needs nurturing. My mother's Remington
tip-tapped through all my childhood fevers, aimed
at realms beyond the sickbed, porch, and yard.
Though Pennsylvania Dutch, she fell in love
with Spain, its wistful knights and Catholic queens
and tried, *tip-tap*, to stretch her Remington
across the gap of space and time, and failed.

I took off from her failure. Katharine White
saw in me fodder for her magazine,
and Judith Jones, from 1960 on,
abetted all my books, an editor
excelling as encourager, who found
the good intention even in a botch.

*

My aspirations met indulgent spirits
long resident in Ink, Inc.'s castle keep:
I somehow wasn't Jewish, which made me
minority and something of a pet.
When Mr. Shawn, the magus in his cave,
went pink, he whispered friendly oracles.
Urbane and dapper Sidney Jacobs, head
of Knopf production, gave a pica stick

to me that I still measure by, and books
of fonts I still consult. Wry Howard Moss
allowed my poems safe passage now and then.
A host of minions supervised my grammar;
a brace of wives forgave my doubtful taste.

*

Today, the author hits three score thirteen,
an age his father, woken in the night
by pressure on his heart, fell short of. Still,
I scribble on. My right hand occupies
the center of my vision, faithful old
five-fingered beast of burden, dappled with
some psoriatic spots I used to hate,
replaced by spots of damage the crude sun-cure

extracted from my dermis through the years.
The beast is dry and mottled, shedding skin
as minutes drop from life, a wristy piece
of dogged ugliness, its labors meant
to carve from language beauty, that beauty which
lifts free of flesh to find itself in print.

My Mother at Her Desk

My mother knew non-publication's shame,
obscurity's abyss, where blind hands flog
typewriter keys in hopes of raising up
the magic combination that will sell.
Instead, brown envelopes return, bent double
in letter slots to flop on the foyer floor,
or else abandoned flat within the tin
of the rural mailbox, as insects whirr.

She studied How To, diagrammed Great Plots
some correspondence course assigned, read Mann,
Flaubert, and Faulkner, looking for the clue,
the "open sesame" to fling the cave door back
and flood with light the shadows in her heart
to turn them golden, worth their weight in cash.

*

Mine was to be the magic gift instead,
propelled to confidence by mother-love
and polished for the New York market by
New England's wintry flair for education.
But hers was the purer ambition, hatched
of country childhood in the silences
of crops accruing, her sole companions birds
whose songs and names she taught herself to know.

Her gray head cocked, she'd say, "The chickadee
feels lonely!" Bent above a book, she'd lift
her still-young face and say, "Such ugly words!"
as if each stood alone. *No, no,* I thought,
context is all. But I was male, and made
to make a mark, while Mother typed birdsong.

Dry Spell, 2006

In Arizona's drought, even cacti
die; the prickly pears are pancake-flat
with no more rain to plump them up, and blanch
to lavender instead of green. Iraq
continues like a curtainless bad play,
the Tucson *Star* headlines the daily bust,
and Barry Bonds limps close to Babe Ruth's record.
Amid all this, I age another notch.

Dear Lord, have I become too poor a thing
to save? My pencil creeps across this page
unsure where next to go. My children phone
from far-off islands, all their lives in flux
while mine has petrified, a desert rock
to take their superstitious bearings by.

*

Today my mate of thirty years and I
explored the grid that fills our foothills view
and bought two oleander plants to screen
our porch from passing cars, or them from us.
How touchingly we scrambled on the rocks,
our footing poor, to pour out Miracle-Gro
(the blue of Listerine) on wilting plants
that mutely guard our island in the sun.

She gave me, at my own discreet request,
a dictionary full of words I keep
forgetting, and a watch whose battery
is guaranteed to last ten years, at least.
Ten years! It will tick in my coffin while
my bones continue to deteriorate.

*

Our view—in other seasons, of the North
Atlantic, luminous and level, fringed
by greenery that goes, all imperceptibly,
from bud to leaf to blaze to cold, bare twig—
at night resembles, in its lateral sweep,
the other one, two thousand miles away.
The city, in its valley lying flat
as golden water, twinkles, ripples, breathes,

streetlights deflected downward to avoid
bleaching the sky for the observatories
whose giant-geared and many-mirrored eyes
peer upward from some local mountaintops.
These mountains hang to the south like blue clouds
that would, back East, past Hull and Hingham, bring rain.

Birthday Shopping, 2007

Today, in Tucson, Mrs. U. and I
drove through the downtown grid, where cowboys in
white pickup trucks turn left against the light,
to Best Buy's big box, to buy a back-up laptop.
Brave world! The geeks in matching shirts
talked gigabytes to girls with blue tattoos
and nostril studs, and guys with ropey arms
packed pixel-rich home-entertainment screens.

Hi-def is in. Attempting to prepare
our obsolescing heads for crashing waves
of new technology, we cruised an aisle
of duplicated, twitching imagery
and came upon, as if upon an elf
asleep on forest moss, a Chinese child.

*

It was a girl, aged two or three, in bangs
and plastic bow and tiny shiny dress
and round-toed Velcroed shoes, supine
upon a cardboard carton, inches from
a coruscating hi-def plasma screen,
her face as close and rapt as at an udder,
motionlessly drinking something in,
an underwater scene of garish fish.

An older sister gazed her fill nearby;
at last we spotted their adoptive ma
haggling fine points several clerks away.
Exquisite in her peace, the alien child
had found a parent, bright and slightly warm,
while I, a birthday boy, was feeling lost.

*

In Pomeroy's Department Store, I lost
my mother's hand three score and more than ten
long years ago. So panicky I wet
my pants a drop or two, I felt space widen;
when someone not my mother took my hand,
I burbled, unable to cough up who
I was, so unforeseeably alone
amid these aisles of goods, so unlike home.

Not so this transfixed little pixie here
among the pixels, stiller than if asleep.
Electromagnetism holds her fast,
secure within the infotainment web,
that sticky and spontaneous conflux
of self-advertisement and spam and porn.

*

Well, even Roosevelt's sunk Depression world—
Atlantis at the bottom of a life,
descried through sliding thicknesses of time—
had radio and cinema to love,
and love we did, in haste to make the new
our own, to wield against our elders, dull
with all the useless stuff they'd had to learn
when they were helpless children just like us.

Signals beyond their ken transported us—
Jack Benny's stately pauses, Errol Flynn's
half-smile, the songs we learned to smoke to, ads
in magazines called slicks, the comic strips,
realer than real, a Paradise that if
we held our breaths, we could ascend to, free.

*

In the beginning, Culture does beguile us,
but Nature gets us in the end. My skin,
I notice now that I am seventy-five,
hangs loose in ripples like those dunes on Mars
that tell us life may have existed there—
monocellular slime in stagnant pools.
After a Tucson movie, some man in
the men's room mirror lunged toward me

with wild small eyes, white hair, and wattled neck—
who could he be, so hostile and so weird,
so due for disposal, like a popcorn bag
vile with its inner film of stale, used grease?
Where was the freckled boy who used to peek
into the front-hall mirror, off to school?

*

Its cracked brown frame and coat of mercury
going thin behind the glass embodied time,
as did the fraying rugs, the kitchen chairs,
the four adults that shared the house with me.
In Pennsylvania then, the past had settled in
to be the present. Nothing greatly changed:
milk came to the porch, and mail through the slot,
coal down the loud chute, and ice in crazed cakes

on the iceman's leathern back. My grandparents
moved through the rooms in a fog of dailiness,
younger then than I am now, and my parents,
not forty—can it be?—expressed their youth
by quarrelling and slamming doors. Our old
clock ticked, and dust, God's pixels, calmly danced.

Spirit of 76

Cypresses have one direction, up,
but sometimes desert zephyrs tousle one
so that a branch or two will stick straight out—
a hatchling fallen from the nest,
a broken leg a limp will not forget,
a lock of cowlicked hair that spurns the comb.
Aspiring like steeples inky green,
they spear the sun-bleached view with nodding tips.

How not to think of death? Its ghastly blank
lies underneath your dreams, that once gave rise
to horn-hard, conscienceless erections.
Just so, your waking brain no longer stiffens
with careless inspirations—urgent news
spilled in clenched spasms on the virgin sheets.

*

Here in this place of arid clarity,
two thousand miles from where my souvenirs
collect a cozy dust, the piled produce
of bald ambition pulling ignorance,
I see clear through to the ultimate page,
the silence I dared break for my small time.
No piece was easy, but each fell finished,
in its shroud of print, into a book-shaped hole.

Be with me, words, a little longer; you
have given me my quitclaim in the sun,
sealed shut my adolescent wounds, made light
of grownup troubles, turned to my advantage
what in most lives would be pure deficit,
and formed, of those I loved, more solid ghosts.

*

Our annual birthday do: dinner at
the Arizona Inn for only two.
White tablecloth, much cutlery, décor
in somber dark-beamed territorial style.
No wine, thank you. Determined to prolong
our second marriages, we gave that up,
with cigarettes. We toast each other's health
in water and a haze of candlelight.

My imitation of a proper man,
white-haired and wed to aging loveliness,
has fit me like a store-bought suit, not quite
my skin, but wearing well enough until,
at ceremony's end, my wife points out
I don't know how to use a finger bowl.

A Lightened Life

Beverly Farms, 04/14/08

A lightened life: last novel proofs FedExed—
the final go-through, back-and-forthing till
all adjectives seemed wrong, inferior to
an almost-glimpsed unreal alternative
spoken perhaps on Mars—and taxes, state
and federal, mailed. They were much more this year,
thanks to the last novel's mild success,
wry fruit of terror-fear and author's tours.

Checks mailed, I stopped for gas, and plumb forgot
how to release the gas-cap door. True,
I'd been driving a rented car for weeks. But, too,
this morning I couldn't do the computer code
for the *accent grave* in *fin-de-siècle,* one
of my favorite words. What's up? What's left of me?

Euonymus 11/02/08

My window tells me the euonymus
arrives now at the last and deepest shade
of red, before its leaves let go. One of
my grandsons leaves a phone message for me;
his voice has deepened. A cold that wouldn't let go
is now a cloud upon my chest X-ray:
pneumonia. My house is now a cage
I prowl, window to window, as I wait

for time to take away the cloud within.
The rusty autumn gold is glorious.
Blue jays and a small gray bird, white-chested,
decline to join the seasonal escape
and flit on bushes below. Is this an end?
I hang, half-healthy, here, and wait to see.

Oblong Ghosts 11/06/08

A wake-up call? It seems that death has found
the portals it will enter by: my lungs,
pathetic oblong ghosts, one paler than
the other on the doctor's viewing screen.
Looking up "pneumonia," I learn
it can, like an erratic dog, turn mean
and snap life short for someone under two
or "very old (over 75)."

Meanwhile, our President Obama waits
downstairs to be unwrapped and I, a child
transposed toward Christmas Day in Shillington—
air soft and bright, a touch of snow outside—
pause here, one hand upon the banister,
and breathe the scent of fresh-cut evergreens.

Hospital 11/23–27/08

Mass. General, Boston

Benign big blond machine beyond all price,
it swallows us up and slowly spits us out
half-deafened and our blood still dyed: all this
to mask the simple dismal fact that we
decay and find our term of life is fixed.
This giant governance, a mammoth toy,
distracts us for the daytime, but the night
brings back the quiet, and the solemn dark.

God save us from ever ending, though billions have.
The world is blanketed by foregone deaths,
small beads of ego, bright with appetite,
whose pin-sized prick of light winked out,
bequeathing Earth a jagged coral shelf
unseen beneath the black unheeding waves.

*

My visitors, my kin. I fall into
the conversational mode, matching it
to each old child, as if we share a joke
(of course we do, the dizzy depths of years),
and each grandchild, politely quizzing them
on their events and prospects, all the while
suppressing, like an acid reflux, the lack
of prospect black and bilious for me.

Must I do this, uphold the social lie
that binds us all together in blind faith
that nothing ends, not youth nor age nor strength,
as in a motion picture which, once seen,
can be rebought on DVD? My tongue
says yes; within, I lamely drown.

*

I think of those I loved and saw to die:
my Grampop in his nightshirt on the floor;
my first wife's mother, unable to take a bite
of Easter dinner, smiling with regret;
my mother in her blue knit cap, alone
on eighty acres, stuck with forty cats,
too weak to walk out to collect the mail,
waving brave goodbye from her wind-chimed porch.

And friends, both male and female, on the phone,
their voices dry and firm, their ends in sight.
My old piano teacher joking, of her latest
diagnosis, "Curtains." I brushed them off,
these valorous, in my unseemly haste
of greedy living, and now must learn from them.

*

Endpoint, I thought, would end a chapter in
a book beyond imagining, that got reset
in crisp exotic type a future I
—a miracle!—could read. My hope was vague
but kept me going, amiable and swift.
A clergyman—those comical purveyors
of what makes sense to just the terrified—
has phoned me, and I loved him, bless his hide.

My wife of thirty years is on the phone.
I get a busy signal, and I know
she's in her grief and needs to organize
consulting friends. But me, I need her voice;
her body is the only locus where
my desolation bumps against its end.

The City Outside 12/11/08

Stirs early: ambulances pull in far
below, unloading steadily their own
emergencies, and stray pedestrians
cross nameless streets. Traffic picks up at dawn,
and lights in the skyscrapers dim.
The map of Beacon Hill becomes 3-D,
a crust of brick and granite, the State House dome
a golden bubble single as the sun.

I lived in Boston once, a year or two,
in furtive semi-bachelorhood. I parked
a Karmann Ghia in Back Bay's shady spots
but I was lighter then, and lived as if
within forever. Now I've turned so heavy
I sink through twenty floors to hit the street.

*

I had a fear of falling—airplanes
spilling their spinning contents like black beans;
the parapets at Rockefeller Center or
the Guggenheim proving too low and sucking
me down with impalpable winds of dread;
engorging atria in swank hotels,
the piano player miles below his music,
his instrument no bigger than a footprint.

I'm safe! Away with travel and abrupt
perspectives! Terra firma is my ground,
my refuge, and my certain destination.
My terrors—the flight through dazzling air, with
the blinding smash, the final black—will be
achieved from thirty inches, on a bed.

*

Strontium 90—is that a so-called
heavy element? I've been injected,
and yet the same light imbecilic stuff—
the babble on TV, newspaper fluff,
the drone of magazines, banality's
kind banter—plows ahead, admixed
with world collapse, atrocities, default,
and fraud. Get off, get off the rotten world!

The sky is turning that pellucid blue
seen in enamel behind a girlish Virgin—
the doeskin lids downcast, the smile demure.
Indigo cloud-shreds dot a band of tan;
the Hancock Tower bares a slice of night.
So whence the world's beauty? Was I deceived?

Peggy Lutz, Fred Muth 12/13/08

They've been in my fiction; both now dead,
Peggy just recently, long stricken (like
my Grandma) with Parkinson's disease.
But what a peppy knockout Peggy was!—
cheerleader, hockey star, May Queen, RN.
Pigtailed in kindergarten, she caught my mother's
eye, but she was too much girl for me.
Fred—so bright, so quietly wry—*his*

mother's eye fell on me, a "nicer" boy
than her son's pet pals. Fred's slight wild streak
was tamed by diabetes. At the end,
it took his toes and feet. Last time we met,
his walk rolled wildly, fetching my coat. With health
he might have soared. As was, he taught me smarts.

*

Dear friends of childhood, classmates, thank you,
scant hundred of you, for providing a
sufficiency of human types: beauty,
bully, hanger-on, natural,
twin, and fatso—all a writer needs,
all there in Shillington, its trolley cars
and little factories, cornfields and trees,
leaf fires, snowflakes, pumpkins, valentines.

To think of you brings tears less caustic
than those the thought of death brings. Perhaps
we meet our heaven at the start and not
the end of life. Even then were tears
and fear and struggle, but the town itself
draped in plain glory the passing days.

*

The town forgave me for existing; it
included me in Christmas carols, songfests
(though I sang poorly) at the Shillington,
the local movie house. My father stood,
in back, too restless to sit, but everybody
knew his name, and mine. In turn I knew
my Granddad in the overalled town crew.
I've written these before, these modest facts,

but their meaning has no bottom in my mind.
The fragments in their jiggled scope collide
to form more sacred windows. I had to move
to beautiful New England—its triple
deckers, whited churches, unplowed streets—
to learn how drear and deadly life can be.

Needle Biopsy 12/22/08

All praise be Valium in Jesus' name:
a CAT-scan needle biopsy sent me
up a happy cul-de-sac, a detour not
detached from consciousness but sweetly part—
I heard machines and experts murmuring about me—
a dulcet tube in which I lay secure and warm
and thought creative thoughts, intensely so,
as in my fading prime. Plans flowered, dreams.

All would be well, I felt, all manner of thing.
The needle, carefully worked, was in me, beyond pain,
aimed at an adrenal gland. I had not hoped
to find, in this bright place, so solvent a peace.
Days later, the results came casually through:
the gland, biopsied, showed metastasis.

Creeper

With what stoic delicacy does
Virginia creeper let go:
the feeblest tug brings down
a sheaf of leaves kite-high,
as if to say, *To live is good*
but not to live—to be pulled down
with scarce a ripping sound,
still flourishing, still
stretching toward the sun—
is good also, all photosynthesis
abandoned, quite quits. Next spring
the hairy rootlets left unpulled
snake out a leafy afterlife
up that same smooth-barked oak.

Fine Point 12/22/08

Why go to Sunday school, though surlily,
and not believe a bit of what was taught?
The desert shepherds in their scratchy robes
undoubtedly existed, and Israel's defeats—
the Temple in its sacredness destroyed
by Babylon and Rome. Yet Jews kept faith
and passed the prayers, the crabbed rites,
from table to table as Christians mocked.

We mocked, but took. The timbrel creed of praise
gives spirit to the daily; blood tinges lips.
The tongue reposes in papyrus pleas,
saying, *Surely*—magnificent, that "surely"—
goodness and mercy shall follow me all
the days of my life, my life, forever.

Notes

The poems are ordered by date of completion. As Updike wrote in a note to his *Collected Poems 1953–1993*, whose contents are ordered on the same principle, "an exact date generally indicates the day of dispatch, when the poem was thought fit to be sent off to a magazine for submission, as duly noted in the upper right corner of my retained copy." With few exceptions, these so-called retained copies are now among the John Updike Papers at Houghton Library, Harvard University, Cambridge, Massachusetts.

Unless he was responding to a request from an editor or institution to commemorate a special occasion ("Seven Stanzas at Easter," "Apologies to Harvard") or treat an assigned topic ("Shillington," "Baseball"), Updike submitted each completed poem to *The New Yorker*, with which he signed a right-of-first-refusal contract in September 1954, at the age of twenty-two. The first readers of almost all the poems collected here were *New Yorker* editors Katharine S. White (1953–58), Howard Moss (1958–87), Alice Quinn (1987–2007), and Paul Muldoon (2007–9).

Updike collected his poems in eight volumes:

THE CARPENTERED HEN *and Other Tame Creatures.* New York: Harper & Row, 1958. ix, 82 pages. (U.K. edition, titled *Hoping for a Hoopoe:* London: Victor Gollancz, 1959.) Second edition, revised and with a foreword by the author: New York: Alfred A. Knopf, 1982. xvii, 84 pages.

TELEPHONE POLES *and Other Poems.* New York: Alfred A. Knopf, 1963. ix, 84 pages. (U.K. edition: London: Andre Deutsch, 1964.)

MIDPOINT *and Other Poems.* New York: Alfred A. Knopf, 1969. viii, 99 pages. (U.K. edition: London: Andre Deutsch, 1969.)

TOSSING AND TURNING. New York: Alfred A. Knopf, 1977. xi, 91 pages. (U.K. edition: London: Andre Deutsch, 1977.)

FACING NATURE. New York: Alfred A. Knopf, 1985. ix, 110 pages. (U.K. edition: London: Andre Deutsch, 1986.)

Collected Poems *1953–1993*, with a preface and notes by the author. New York: Alfred A. Knopf, 1993. xxiv, 387 pages. (U.K. edition: London: Hamish Hamilton, 1993.)

Americana *and Other Poems.* New York: Alfred A. Knopf, 2001. xi, 95 pages. (U.K. edition: London: Penguin Books, 2001.)

Endpoint *and Other Poems.* New York: Alfred A. Knopf, 2009. xi, 97 pages. (U.K. edition: London: Hamish Hamilton, 2009.)

Poems collected in the first six volumes are printed as they appeared in the corrected Knopf paperback printing of *Collected Poems* (July 1995), whose texts Updike deemed definitive. Poems first collected in *Americana* and *Endpoint* are printed as they appeared in the first Knopf printings (May 2001 and April 2009, respectively). Exceptions to these rules, and sources for the texts of previously unpublished and uncollected poems, are detailed below.

The editor wishes to thank Leslie Morris and Heather Cole, of Houghton Library, for facilitating his work among the John Updike Papers. Kristin Cook, of the Boston Athenæum, helped him in his bibliographic research.

For further information about the publication history of these poems than is given in the following notes, see Jack De Bellis and Michael Broomfield, *John Updike: A Bibliography of Primary and Secondary Materials, 1948–2007* (New Castle, Delaware: Oak Knoll Press, 2008).

In the notes below, line counts do not include titles, subheadings, or stanza breaks. Quotations from Shakespeare are keyed to G. Blakemore Evans, editor, *The Riverside Shakespeare* (Boston: Houghton Mifflin, 1974). Quotations from the Bible are keyed to the King James Version.

Why the Telephone Wires Dip and the Poles Are Cracked and Crooked (p. 3)

Completed in the spring or early summer of 1953. Published, under the heading "Footnotes to the Future," in *The Harvard Lampoon* 142:7 (October 1953), p. 14. Reprinted in *The Carpentered Hen* (1958), p. 9, and *Collected Poems* (1993), p. 3.

In the preface to *Collected Poems,* Updike wrote that this early poem, "bearing a comically long title, yet conveyed, with a compression unprecedented in my brief writing career, the mythogenetic truth of telephone wires and poles marching across a stretch of Pennsylvania farmland. I still remember the shudder, the triumphant sense of capture, with which I got these lines down, not long after my twenty-first birthday."

Coming into New York (p. 4)

Completed June 25, 1953. Found by the editor, in fair-copy typescript, among Updike's "Harvard Poems," four folders of unpublished verse written between the author's graduation from high school (June 1950) and his graduation from college (June 1954), now in the John Updike Papers (MS Am 1793 [261]).

Ex–Basketball Player (p. 5)

Completed July 5, 1954. Published in *The New Yorker* 33:20 (July 6, 1957), p. 62. Reprinted in *The Carpentered Hen* (1958), pp. 2–3, and *Collected Poems* (1993), pp. 4–5.

Updike's note in *Collected Poems* reads: "My only oft-anthologized poem. The second stanza receives footnotes in some textbooks, to explain that once upon a time a gasoline station might offer a variety of brands of gasoline, with the trade names identified on glass heads above the pumps, and that ESSO, predecessor of EXXON, was one of the brands. The crowdlike candies are behind the luncheonette counter, beyond reach."

Sunflower (p. 6)

Completed August 30, 1954. Published in *The New Yorker* 31:30 (September 10, 1955), p. 136. Reprinted in *The Carpentered Hen* (1958), p. 21, and *Collected Poems* (1993), pp. 6–7.

Burning Trash (p. 7)

Completed March 22, 1955. Published in *The New Yorker* 68:42 (December 7, 1992), p. 92. Reprinted in *Collected Poems* (1993), p. 9.

Tao in the Yankee Stadium Bleachers (p. 8)

Completed in the spring of 1956. Published in *The New Yorker* 32:26 (August 18, 1956), p. 28. Reprinted in *The Carpentered Hen* (1958), pp. 52–53, and *Collected Poems* (1993), pp. 10–11.

The poem appeared in *The New Yorker* with the subtitle "What Comes of Reading Chuang-tzu Between Innings" but was reprinted in *The Carpentered Hen* without it. The present subtitle appeared in the revised, twenty-fifth-anniversary edition of *The Carpentered Hen* (1982) but not in *Collected Poems. Three Ways of Thought in Ancient China* (London: Allen & Unwin, 1939), a selection of extracts from Chuang-tzu, Mencius, and Han Fei-tzu, was edited, translated, and annotated by the British sinologist Arthur Waley (1889–1966). Updike owned the Doubleday Anchor paperback edition of 1956.

Shillington (p. 9)

Completed January 15, 1958, having been commissioned in the fall of 1957 by Charles J. Hemmig, editor of *Fifty Years of Progress, 1908–1958: Shillington, Pennsylvania,* a publication of Shillington's Fiftieth Anniversary General Committee. (Shillington, today a suburb of Reading, was incorporated as a borough on August 18, 1908.) Published, as "My Home Town," in *Fifty Years of Progress* (1958), p. 11, and in *Historical Review of Berks County* 24:2 (Spring 1959), p. 57. Reprinted, under the present title, in *Telephone Poles* (1963), p. 60, and *Collected Poems* (1993), p. 15.

For Updike's biographical sketch of Mr. Hemmig, see the seventh stanza of "In the Cemetery High Above Shillington" (p. 167 of the present volume).

Mobile of Birds (p. 10)

Completed August 16, 1958. Published in *The New Yorker* 35:44 (December 19, 1959), p. 32. Reprinted in *Telephone Poles* (1963), pp. 66–67, and *Collected Poems* (1993), p. 14.

Updike's note in *Collected Poems* reads: "Perhaps the same mobile evoked in the short story 'Toward Evening,' which was brought home by the young New Yorker, Rafe, to his wife and infant daughter: 'The mobile was not a success. Alice had expected a genuine Calder, made of beautiful polished woods, instead of seven rubber birds, with celluloid wings, hung from a piece of coarse wire. Elizabeth wanted to put the birds in her mouth and showed no interest in, perhaps did not even see, their abstract swinging, quite unlike the rapt infant shown on the box.' "

Telephone Poles (p. 11)

Completed June 20, 1959. Published in *The New Yorker* 36:49 (January 21, 1961), p. 36. Reprinted in *Telephone Poles* (1963), p. 43, and *Collected Poems* (1993), pp. 16–17.

Modigliani's Death Mask (p. 12)

Completed November 25, 1959. Published in *The New Yorker* 36:6 (March 26, 1960), p. 34. Reprinted in *Telephone Poles* (1963), p. 75, and *Collected Poems* (1993), p. 19.

A white plaster death mask of the Italian artist Amedeo Modigliani (1884–1920), made by his friends Conrad Moricand and Moïse Kisling, has been in the collection of the Harvard Art Museums since 1929. This mask provided the basis for a bronze sculpture by Modigliani's admirer Jacques Lipchitz, designed and cast in the spring of 1920.

Seagulls (p. 13)

Completed December 5, 1959. Published in *The New Yorker* 38:27 (August 25, 1962), p. 28. Reprinted in *Telephone Poles* (1963), pp. 50–51, and *Collected Poems* (1993), pp. 19–20.

In a contribution to *Poetspeak*, a creative-writing textbook edited by Paul B. Janeczko (Scarsdale, New York: Bradbury Press, 1983), Updike recounted the moment of inspiration for "Seagulls": "I was lying on the beach in Ipswich, Massachusetts, in the very late afternoon of a summer or early fall day in 1959. As the beach crowds thinned, the seagulls moved closer, and while I lay on my side, observing one, the first lines of this poem came to me. . . . The form is, the student will notice, unrhymed 'free' verse; but I wrote much light verse in regular meters in those days, and the ghosts of rhyme and stanza in my ear helped press my lines toward the crispness that must exist in poetry. The second stanza always gets a laugh when I read it aloud, but I was not consciously intending to be funny when I wrote it—merely exact. I, too, felt ugly because I was intelligent, and as I settled into my writer's profession well aware of my 'wide and nervous and well-muscled rump.' The subject, in short, leaped to my heart with unforced self-symbolic import."

Updike's contribution to *Poetspeak* was reprinted in full in his nonfiction collection *Hugging the Shore* (New York: Knopf, 1983), pp. 865–66.

Seven Stanzas at Easter (p. 15)

Completed January 10, 1960. Printed in the bulletin of Clifton Lutheran Church, Marblehead, Massachusetts, for April 17, 1960. Published in *The Christian Century* 78:8 (February 22, 1961), p. 236. Reprinted in *Telephone Poles* (1963), pp. 72–73, and *Collected Poems* (1993), pp. 20–21.

Updike's note in *Collected Poems* reads: "Composed for a religious arts festival sponsored by the Clifton Lutheran Church, of Marblehead, Massachusetts, which I sometimes attended. Norman Kretzmann was pastor. Gratifyingly, the poem won first prize and has figured in a number of neo-orthodox sermons."

B.W.I. (p. 16)

Completed February 1960. Published in *The New Yorker* 36:11 (April 30, 1960), p. 98. Reprinted in *Telephone Poles* (1963), p. 21, and *Collected Poems* (1993), p. 22.

Updike's note in *Collected Poems* reads, in part: "Composed on the island of Anguilla, while lying on a dark Edwardian sofa, where I wrote during [six] weeks of tropical sabbatical."

February 22 (p. 17)

Completed February 28, 1960. Published in *The New Yorker* 37:1 (February 18, 1961), p. 40. Reprinted in *Telephone Poles* (1963), pp. 58–59, and *Collected Poems* (1993), p. 23.

Vermont (p. 18)

Completed September 5, 1960. Published in *Harper's* 223:1334 (July 1961), p. 67. Reprinted in *Telephone Poles* (1963), p. 53, and *Collected Poems* (1993), p. 26.

Updike drafted this poem in South Duxbury, Vermont, at the summer home of his father-in-law, the Chicago-based Unitarian minister Leslie T. Pennington.

Fever (p. 19)

Completed March 24, 1961. Published in *Telephone Poles* (1963), p. 71, and reprinted in *Collected Poems* (1993), p. 28.

Earthworm (p. 20)

Completed May 2, 1961. Published in *The New Yorker* 38:12 (May 12, 1962), p. 145. Reprinted in *Telephone Poles* (1963), p. 48, and *Collected Poems* (1993), p. 29.

Updike told James Yerkes, the editor of *John Updike and Religion* (Grand Rapids: Eerdmans, 1999), that this poem is "perhaps my best-felt statement on religion." At Updike's request, it and an abridged version of "Seven Stanzas at Easter" (p. 15) were read at his funeral.

Boil (p. 21)

Completed February 7, 1962. Printed in *Bits 5*, one of a series of semi-annual poetry pamphlets edited and printed by Updike's Harvard classmate Robert Wallace (Cleveland: Bits Press, 1977), p. 4. Reprinted in *Tossing and Turning* (1977), p. 86, and *Collected Poems* (1993), p. 33.

My Children at the Dump (p. 22)

Completed October 23, 1962. Published, as "My Children at the Dump at Ipswich," in *The Transatlantic Review* 14 (Autumn 1963), p. 70. Reprinted, under the present title, in *Midpoint* (1969), pp. 70–71, and *Collected Poems* (1993), pp. 35–36.

The Great Scarf of Birds (p. 23)

Completed October 25, 1962. Published in *The New Yorker* 38:36 (October 27, 1962), p. 52. Reprinted in *Telephone Poles* (1963), pp. 82–83, and *Collected Poems* (1993), pp. 37–38.

When revising this poem for *Collected Poems*, Updike abridged the text as it had appeared in *Telephone Poles* and later regretted the results. In his office copy of *Collected Poems* he restored most of the cuts, notably the first and final stanzas. These restorations are honored here.

Hoeing (p. 25)

Completed April 27, 1963. Published in *The New Yorker* 39:10 (April 27, 1963), p. 142. Reprinted in *Telephone Poles* (1963), p. 54, and *Collected Poems* (1993), pp. 40–41.

Fireworks (p. 26)

Completed July 5, 1963. Published in *The New Yorker* 40:20 (July 4, 1964), p. 28. Reprinted in *Midpoint* (1969), p. 47, and *Collected Poems* (1993), pp. 42–43.

from *Postcards from Soviet Cities* (p. 27)

Written October–November 1964, during a six-week tour of the Soviet Union sponsored by the U.S. State Department. Published in *The New Yorker* 41:15 (May 29, 1965), p. 34. Reprinted, together with a fifth and penultimately positioned postcard, "Tbilisi," in *Midpoint* (1969), pp. 84–87, and *Collected Poems* (1993), pp. 45–48. *The New Yorker*'s group of four postcards is used here, and the *Collected Poems* texts.

Moscow, line 6: In *Collected Poems*, Updike glossed "GUM" as "the great emporium on Red Square, an acronym for 'Gosudarstvyenni Universalni Magazin' (State Universal Department Store)."

Leningrad: Forty-four years later, during a late-life trip to Russia, Updike wrote a post-Soviet sequel to this postcard. The sonnet "St. Petersburg," completed September 25, 2008, was published, posthumously, in *Endpoint:*

Acres of gold leaf, feathered into place
with squirrel tails, restored the palaces
for tourist trade. Tremendous churches, freed
from gray decades of Marxist usefulness
as barracks, atheist museums, or
warehouses for potatoes and state goods,
proclaim again the news of risen Christ
in marble, malachite, and candlelight.

Peter the Great applied to muddy marsh
alive with estuary currents stones
that paved relentless streets Italianate
in pastel tints and pillared pomp. Lean girls
in tall and pricey boots now stalk soft prey
where their grandmothers starved on hard Siege-bread.

Line 1: St. Petersburg's epithet "a window on the west" was popularized by Pushkin in the opening stanza of his *Bronze Horseman* (1837).

Kiev, lines 1–4: A monument topped by a sixty-foot statue of St. Vladimir (1853) dominates Kiev's St. Michael's Park.

Line 14, "Moussorgsky's Gate": "The Great Gate of Kiev" is the tenth movement of Modest Moussorgsky's piano suite *Pictures at an Exhibition* (1874).

Roman Portrait Busts (p. 30)

Completed December 30, 1964. Published in *The New Republic* 152:6 (February 6, 1965), p. 21. Reprinted in *Midpoint* (1969), p. 59, and *Collected Poems* (1993), p. 49.

Dog's Death (p. 31)

Completed March 16, 1965. Printed as a broadside, in an edition limited to a hundred copies signed by the author (Cambridge, Massachusetts: The Adams House and Lowell House Printers, Harvard Yard, May 1965). Reprinted in *Midpoint* (1969), p. 52, and *Collected Poems* (1993), pp. 51–52.

Updike's note in *Collected Poems* reads: "The dog's name was Polly; she didn't live with us on East Street [Ipswich] very long. Sometimes it seems the whole purpose of pets is to bring death into the house."

Memories of Anguilla, 1960 (p. 32)

Completed in the summer of 1967. Published, under the present title, in *The New Republic* 157:20 (November 11, 1967), p. 21. Reprinted without title, as part of the "P.S." to the journalistic "Letter from Anguilla," in Updike's nonfiction collection *Picked-Up Pieces* (New York: Knopf, 1975), pp. 78–79. The text from *Picked-Up Pieces* is used here.

Line 2, "Tilley lamps": Pressurized kerosene lamps widely used throughout the former British Empire. They are named after their original manufacturer, William H. Tilley, who popularized them in London after 1818.

Topsfield Fair (p. 34)

Completed September 25, 1967. Published in *The American Scholar* 37:3 (Summer 1968), p. 419. Reprinted in *Midpoint* (1969), p. 51, and *Collected Poems* (1993), p. 61.

Topsfield Fair is an agricultural exhibition, held most every fall since 1820 in the town of Topsfield, in Essex County, Massachusetts.

Dream Objects (p. 35)

Completed June 10, 1968. Published in *The New Yorker* 44:36 (October 26, 1968), p. 54. Reprinted in *Midpoint* (1969), p. 55, and *Collected Poems* (1993), pp. 63–64.

Midpoint (p. 36)

Written April–August 1968. Canto III, "The Dance of the Solids," was published in *Scientific American* 200:1 (January 1969), pp. 130–31. The complete poem was published in *Midpoint* (1969), pp. 3–44, and reprinted in *Collected Poems* (1993), pp. 64–101.

For the jacket flap of *Midpoint*, Updike wrote the following abstract: "In the boldly eclectic title poem of this collection, John Updike employs the meters of Dante, Spenser, Pope, Whitman, and Pound, as well as the pictographic tactics of concrete poetry, to take an inventory of his life at the end of his thirty-fifth year—at midpoint. These cantos form both a joke on the antique genre of the long poem and an attempt to write one: an earnest meditation on the mysteries of the ego, lost time, and the mundane."

Updike's notes from *Collected Poems* read as follows:

Canto I, line 174, "still alive . . .": "My father died in April 1972, at the age of seventy-two [see 'The House Growing,' p. 84]; my mother in October 1989, at the age of eighty-five [see 'Fall,' p. 148]."

Canto I, line 181, "From *Time*'s grim cover . . .": "Issue of April 26, 1968."

Canto II, page 48: "The two fine-grained portraits appeared, top, in the *Register* for Harvard's freshman class [fall 1950] and, bottom, four years later, in the yearbook for the graduating class [spring 1954]."

Canto II, page 49, bottom: "Two pictures of the same baby"—Updike's first child, Elizabeth Pennington Updike, born in Oxford, England, on April 1, 1955.

"Canto III was closely based upon the September 1967 issue of *Scientific American*, devoted to 'Materials.'

"In Canto IV, almost all of the quotations are from Walt Whitman's 'Song of Myself.' The prose 'his eyes shut . . . eye in it' is from the last chapter of James Joyce's *Ulysses*, referring not to Bloom but to Lieutenant Mulvey, on the Rock of Gibraltar. The marginal quotation 'the ant's . . . world" is from Ezra Pound's *Cantos*, Canto LXXXI. 'The garden . . . south' is from Theodore Roethke's 'She.'"

Additional notes by the editor follow:

Canto IV, line 30, "CLEAN GENE": Nickname given Senator Eugene McCarthy (D–Minn.) during his unsuccessful presidential campaign of 1968.

Canto IV, line 85, "fox-in-the-morning": In his novel *Rabbit at Rest* (1990), Updike recalls the rules of this playground game: "You all lined up on one side of the asphalt. . . . One person was 'it,' and that one would call out 'Fox in the morning,' and you would all run to the other side, and 'it' would grab one victim from the running throng and drag him or her into the circle painted on the asphalt, and then there would be two 'it's, and these would capture two more on the next massed gallop from safety to safety, and these four would become eight, and soon a whole mob would be roving the center; the proportions were reversed. The last person left uncaught became 'it' for the next game."

Canto IV, line 184, "Cocteau movie": *The Testament of Orpheus* (1960).

Canto IV, lines 185–86, "Gloucester's / 'vile jelly'": *King Lear*, III.vii.82.

Canto IV, lines 297–98, "a drowning man . . . his own hair": See Karl Barth, "He Stands by Us" (1958), in his collection of sermons *Deliverance to the Captives*, translated from the German by Marguerite Wieser (New York: Harper & Row, 1961).

Canto V, line 161, "The Wisdom of the Earth is Foolishness": cf. 1 Corinthians 3:19.

Canto V, line 162, "Chilmark Pond": On Martha's Vineyard.

Living with a Wife (p. 74)

Completed February 26, 1969. Published in *Crazy Horse* 10 (May 1972), pp. 37–39. Reprinted in *Tossing and Turning* (1977), pp. 68–70, and *Collected Poems* (1993), pp. 103–5.

Updike's note in *Collected Poems* reads: "Composed, evidently, the year we lived in London, at 59 Cumberland Terrace, though the imagery is all-American—except, possibly, for the bathtub. My wife did much of our wash in it, the washing machine having never worked, though we were paying a princely rent."

Under the Sunlamp, line 6, *"Urfreude"*: Nietzsche's "primal joy."

Tossing and Turning (p. 77)

Completed November 17, 1969. Published in *The New York Quarterly* 3 (Summer 1970), p. 14. Reprinted in *Tossing and Turning* (1977), p. 67, and *Collected Poems* (1993), pp. 109–10.

On an Island (p. 78)

Completed February 24, 1970. Published in *Saturday Review* 53:45 (November 7, 1970), p. 29. Reprinted in *Tossing and Turning* (1977), pp. 20–21, and *Collected Poems* (1993), pp. 110–11.

Updike's note in *Collected Poems* identifies the island as "Tortola, in the British Virgins."

Marching Through a Novel (p. 79)

Completed September 8, 1970. Published in *Saturday Review* 54:27 (July 3, 1971), p. 24. Reprinted in *Tossing and Turning* (1977), p. 71, and *Collected Poems* (1993), pp. 111–12.

Updike's note in *Collected Poems* identifies the novel as *Rabbit Redux* (1971).

Three Poems from Airplanes (p. 80)

Written 1964–70. Submitted September 15, 1970, to L. E. Sissman, poetry editor of *Bostonian* magazine, a short-lived monthly modeled on *The New Yorker*. Published in *Bostonian* 1:3 (March 1971), p. 37.

Commuter Hop: Completed, as "From an Airplane, in April," on April 2, 1964. Published, as "The Shuttle," in *Bostonian* (see above). The present text and title come from a draft prepared for, but in the end omitted from, *Collected Poems* (John Updike Papers, MS Am 1793 [2835]).

Above What God Sees: Completed December 14, 1964. Published in *Bostonian* (see above), the source of the text used here.

Night Flight, over Ocean: Completed September 15, 1970. Published in *Bostonian* (see above). Reprinted in *Tossing and Turning* (1977), p. 72, and *Collected Poems* (1993), p. 112. The text from *Collected Poems* is used here.

These three poems are representative of the several that Updike composed while "high above the earth, gazing out of airplane windows at a level of global reality unseen until this [the twentieth] century." Here is a fourth such—the sonnet "From Above," completed January 23, 1986, published later that year in *Ontario Review*. The text is reprinted from *Collected Poems*.

These pink-white acres of overcast
have rivers and cliffs, seen from above.
A heavenly sight, such vapor grazed
by sunset-red; interstices
show baby-blue, a shadow of
the hazed and hidden earth.
Dead-level with our eyes, a horizon
of buff, a salmon line, defines

a smooth electric firmament—
a second sky we fliers see.
Leonardo, Bellini, and others arisen
as Christendom evaporated
first caught that tint, that cold blue-green
just there, where illusion ends.

Phenomena (p. 82)

Completed May 20, 1971. Published in *The New Yorker* 49:1 (February 24, 1973), p. 38. Reprinted in *Tossing and Turning* (1977), pp. 84–85, and *Collected Poems* (1993), pp. 113–14.

Updike's note in *Collected Poems* is a comment on the poem's first line: "We had moved to 50 Labor-in-Vain Road [Ipswich], on a tidal inlet called Labor-in-Vain Creek."

The House Growing (p. 84)

Completed April 28, 1972. Published in *The New Yorker* 49:22 (July 23, 1973), p. 34. Reprinted in *Tossing and Turning* (1977), p. 12, and *Collected Poems* (1993), p. 116.

The "old house" of the poem is the Hoyer family's sandstone farmhouse in Plowville, Pennsylvania. Updike lived there for five years—from November 1945 until his departure for Harvard in August 1950—with his father, mother, and maternal grandfather (d. 1953) and grandmother (d. 1955). Updike's father, Wesley Russell Updike, died on April 16, 1972, at the age of seventy-two.

Apologies to Harvard (p. 85)

Completed in early June 1973. Delivered, as the annual Phi Beta Kappa poem, to the Harvard and Radcliffe chapters of Phi Beta Kappa, in Sanders Theatre, Cambridge, Massachusetts, on June 12, 1973. Published in *The Harvard Bulletin* 75:11 (July 1973), pp. 22–23. Reprinted in *Tossing and Turning* (1977), pp. 29–34, and *Collected Poems* (1993), pp. 120–25.

Updike's note in *Collected Poems* reads, in part: "Composed under the clear influence of L. E. Sissman, whose . . . own Phi Beta Kappa poem, the beautiful 'Temporary Measures,' had been delivered two years earlier."

Line 7, "Richardson's stout brown": American architect Henry Hobson Richardson (1838–1886) designed Sever Hall (1878–80), a brown brick Romanesque classroom building in Harvard Yard.

Line 8, "Puseyite cement": Nathan Marsh Pusey (1907–2001) was president of Harvard University from 1953 to 1971.

Line 60, "Dr. Havelock": London-born classicist Eric Havelock (1903–1988) was a professor of Greek and Latin at Harvard from 1947 to 1963.

Line 142, "Royce and William James": Harvard professors Josiah Royce (1855–1916) and William James (1842–1910) together towered over American philosophy and religious thought during the late nineteenth and early twentieth centuries.

Heading for Nandi (p. 90)

Completed March 8, 1974. Published in *The New Yorker* 50:43 (December 16, 1974), p. 42. Reprinted in *Tossing and Turning* (1977), pp. 90–91, and *Collected Poems* (1993), pp. 128–29.

Updike's note in *Collected Poems* reads, in part: "When this appeared in *The New Yorker*, several letters protested that that place was called Nadi. But it was identified as Nandi in the Honolulu airport, and if it had been called Nadi I wouldn't have written the poem." Updike also identifies Fayaway (line 22) as "Melville's lovely native companion in *Typee* [1846]."

Golfers (p. 92)

Completed February 28, 1975. Published in *The New Republic* 172:14 (April 5, 1975), p. 30. Reprinted in *Tossing and Turning* (1977), p. 73, *Collected Poems* (1993), p. 133, and *Golf Dreams: Writings on Golf* (New York: Knopf, 1996), p. 143. The text from *Collected Poems* is used here.

Poisoned in Nassau (p. 93)

Completed March 3, 1975. Published in *Boston University Journal* 23:3 (Fall 1975), p. 48. Reprinted in *Tossing and Turning* (1977), p. 23, and *Collected Poems* (1993), pp. 133–34.

Leaving Church Early (p. 94)

Completed December 1975. Published in *Ontario Review* 5 (Fall/Winter 1976/77), pp. 14–17. Reprinted in *Tossing and Turning* (1977), pp. 7–11, and *Collected Poems* (1993), pp. 137–41.

In *Collected Poems,* Updike wrote of lines 48–49: "My dear grandmother, Katie Hoyer, in her seventies at this time, suffered from Parkinson's disease and often could not get her speech organs working. My mother called this poem 'harsh,' and now I see what she meant; an adolescent harshness is part of the picture."

Line 88, "Nero Wolfe": Detective hero of dozens of whodunits by Rex Stout (1886–1975). He raised orchids on the top floor of his West Thirty-fifth Street townhouse.

In *Collected Poems,* Updike wrote of lines 98–99: "The 'incongruous painting,' by Alice W. Davis in 1933, of the Provincetown dunes, now [sixty years later, in 1993] rests on my third floor [in Beverly Farms, Massachusetts], which has a view of the 'unattainable sea.' I wonder if the painting, our landlocked family's most precious work of art, got me to the New England shore." The painting was later the subject of Updike's essay "An Oil on Canvas" (2004), and is reproduced, as a full-color frontispiece to the essay, on page x of his book *Still Looking: Essays on American Art* (Knopf, 2005).

Another Dog's Death (p. 99)

Completed January 5, 1976. Published in *New England Monthly* 2:1 (January 1985), p. 76. Reprinted in *Facing Nature* (1985), p. 57, and *Collected Poems* (1993), pp. 141–42.

Updike's note in *Collected Poems* identifies the dog as "Helen, a golden retriever and family pet for many years."

Dream and Reality (p. 100)

Completed March 5, 1976. Published in *The New Yorker* 52:49 (January 24, 1977), p. 34. Reprinted in *Tossing and Turning* (1977), pp. 4–5, and *Collected Poems* (1993), pp. 142–43.

Line 27: Diamond type is tiny, only 4.5 points high.

Dutch Cleanser (p. 101)

Completed March 11, 1976. Published in *The Paris Review* 68 (Winter 1976), p. 57. Reprinted in *Tossing and Turning* (1977), p. 89, and *Collected Poems* (1993), pp. 143–44.

Line 16, *"Deutsche Grossmutter":* German grandmother.

Rats (p. 102)

Completed October 22, 1976. Published in *The Atlantic* 239:2 (February 1977), p. 34. Reprinted in *Tossing and Turning* (1977), p. 65, and *Collected Poems* (1993), p. 144.

Calder's Hands (p. 103)

Completed November 14, 1976. Published in *The New Yorker* 52:42 (December 6, 1976), p. 45. Reprinted in *Tossing and Turning* (1977), p. 40, and *Collected Poems* (1993), p. 146.

Alexander Calder died on November 11, 1976, about a month after the opening of *Calder's Universe*, a retrospective exhibition at the Whitney Museum of American Art.

Spanish Sonnets (p. 104)

Completed April 29, 1977. Published in *The New Yorker* 54:23 (July 24, 1978), p. 25. Reprinted in *Facing Nature* (1985), pp. 17–24, and *Collected Poems* (1993), pp. 147–51.

The Goyas alluded to in Sonnet II—*La Familia de Carlos IV* (c. 1800) and *El Perro Semi-hundido* (c. 1819–23)—are in the collection of the Museo Nacional del Prado, Madrid.

The italicized Spanish words in Sonnet VI translate as "Punctured tire" and "Miracle!"

In *Collected Poems,* Updike published the following notes on Sonnet VIII:

Line 2, "Joanna the Mad": "In Spanish, Juana la Loca (1479–1555): the third child of Ferdinand and Isabella, she inherited the thrones of Castile (in 1504) and Aragon (in 1516) through the deaths of the precedent heirs and the ambitions of her husband, Philip the Handsome of Habsburg. After her husband's unexpected death in 1506, her mental imbalance passed into insanity, and in 1509 she retired to Tordesillas, where she lived in squalor, under guard, with the embalmed corpse of her husband. She was the mother of the Emperor Charles V."

Line 6, "Alvaro de Luna": "The able favorite of the inept John II of Castile, de Luna was executed in 1453, after thirty years of dominating the throne and directing its prerogatives toward his own aggrandizement. According to William H. Prescott's *History of the Reign of Ferdinand and Isabella*, 'As he ascended the scaffold, he surveyed the apparatus of death with composure, and calmly submitted himself to the stroke of the executioner, who, in the savage style of the executions of that day, plunged his knife into the throat of his victim, and deliberately severed his head from his body.' The king, who did not long outlive his favorite, would have countermanded the execution but for the steely insistence of his queen, Isabella, the granddaughter of the monarch of Portugal and the mother of the more famous Isabella. It had been de Luna, ironically, who had arranged the marriage, against John II's own inclination to marry a French princess."

To Ed Sissman (p. 108)

Completed September 20, 1977. Published in *Ontario Review* 9 (Fall/Winter, 1978/79), pp. 19–20. Reprinted in *Facing Nature* (1985), pp. 3–5, and *Collected Poems* (1993), pp. 151–53.

The poet L. E. (Louis Edward) Sissman died, from Hodgkin's disease, on March 10, 1976, at the age of forty-eight.

In *Collected Poems,* Updike commented on line 5 of Sonnet I: "Josèph's, long gone, was in the Seventies the premier eating-spot in Boston. The accented second syllable was part of its panache."

For more of Updike on Sissman, see his *New Yorker* obituary, collected in *Higher Gossip* (New York: Knopf, 2011), pp. 77–78, and his essays "Sissman's Prose" and "Sissman's Poetry," in *Hugging the Shore* (New York: Knopf, 1983), pp. 627–34.

On the Way to Delphi (p. 110)

Completed November 19, 1978. Published in *The New Republic* 180:25 (June 23, 1979), p. 34. Reprinted in *Facing Nature* (1985), p. 68, and *Collected Poems* (1993), p. 156.

Crab Crack (p. 111)

Completed September 5, 1980. Published in *Harper's* 263:1574 (July 1981), p. 80. Reprinted in *Facing Nature* (1985), pp. 58–59, and *Collected Poems* (1993), pp. 163–64.

The Moons of Jupiter (p. 113)

Completed January 3, 1981. Published in *The American Scholar* 51:4 (Autumn 1982), pp. 483–86. Reprinted in *Facing Nature* (1985), pp. 71–74, and *Collected Poems* (1993), pp. 165–68.

Updike was fascinated by NASA's Voyager mission to the outer planets, and by the images the twin spacecraft beamed back to Pasadena. This poem draws heavily on information published in the illustrated articles "The Galilean Moons of Jupiter," by Laurence A. Soderblom, *Scientific American* 242:1 (January 1980), and "What Voyager Saw: Jupiter's Dazzling Realm," by Rick Gore, *National Geographic* 157:1 (January 1980).

Updike's notes in *Collected Poems* read, in part:

"Should this be classed as light verse . . . ? . . . 'The Moons of Jupiter' derives from, to quote my own criterion, 'the man-made world of information.' But the poem also derives from the real, and brings back things seen and felt—the unjust parental slap, the sneering note passed hand to hand in a classroom, the punch given back to the ribs of the opposing body, the love of excrement, and the cosmic acrophobia of the last stanza."

Line 106, "enormity": "Used in its preferred sense of, as Webster says, 'a grave offense against order, right, or decency,' with a pun upon its secondary, semi-literate, and increasingly common sense of 'enormousness.'"

Upon the Last Day of His Forty-Ninth Year (p. 117)

Completed March 19, 1981. Published, as "Upon the Last Day of His Forty-Eighth Year," in *The New Republic* 184:20 (May 16, 1981), p. 30. Reprinted in *Facing Nature* (1985), p. 10, and *Collected Poems* (1993), p. 169.

In a note in *Collected Poems*, Updike, commenting on the title, writes that the poem was composed as "I was about to turn forty-nine and enter my fiftieth year. My fiftieth birthday was hedged with so much ceremony as to muffle the terror."

Small-City People (p. 118)

Completed December 18, 1981. Printed as a broadside, in an edition of a hundred copies signed by the author (Northridge, California: Lord John Press, 1982). Reprinted in *Facing Nature* (1985), pp. 46–47, and *Collected Poems* (1993), pp. 174–75.

Updike's note in *Collected Poems* reads: "Inspired by Lawrence, Massachusetts, a city my occasional visits to have inspired urban furniture for the short story 'More Stately Mansions' and the novel *Memories of the Ford Administration*. The poem 'July' [p. 156] came to me in the stately park there. Lawrence reminds me of Reading, Pennsylvania, a city where I always feel excited and childlike."

Plow Cemetery (p. 120)

Completed February 18, 1982. Published in *Antæus* 47 (Autumn 1982), pp. 95–96. Reprinted in *Facing Nature* (1985), pp. 32–34, and *Collected Poems* (1993), pp. 176–77.

Line 27, *"Hier ruhe"*: Here rests.

Styles of Bloom (p. 122)

Completed May 30, 1982. Printed both as a broadside, in an edition of eighty-one copies signed by the author, and as the second poem in *Spring Trio*, by John Updike, a chapbook of three previously unpublished poems, in an edition of 150 copies signed by the author (Winston-Salem, North Carolina: Palæmon Press, 1982). Reprinted in *Facing Nature* (1985), p. 28, and *Collected Poems* (1993), p. 180.

Two Hoppers (p. 123)

Completed August 20, 1982. Published, as "Two Hoppers on Display at the National Gallery," in *The New Republic* 188:4 (January 31, 1983), p. 35. Reprinted in *Facing Nature* (1985), p. 49, and *Collected Poems* (1993), p. 181.

Girl at a Sewing Machine (1921) and *Hotel Room* (1931) were among the canvases shown in *Twentieth-Century Masters*, a touring exhibition of paintings from the private collection of Baron Hans Heinrich Thyssen-Bornemisza, on view at the National Gallery, Washington, D.C., from May 30 to September 8, 1982.

The Code (p. 124)

Completed April 24, 1983. Published in *Ontario Review* 20 (Spring/Summer 1984), p. 34. Reprinted in *Facing Nature* (1985), p. 40, and *Collected Poems* (1993), p. 185.

Richmond (p. 125)

Completed November 28, 1983. Published in *Facing Nature* (1985), p. 13, and reprinted in *Collected Poems* (1993), p. 189.

Line 11, "a set of scattered tombs": The Museum of Edgar Allan Poe, established 1922, comprises three buildings on Richmond's Main Street—the Old Stone House (for Poe's personal effects), the Model Building (for the eighteen-foot model of the early-nineteenth-century city), and a building for temporary exhibits.

Line 14, "Virginia": Poe's wife, the former Virginia Eliza Clemm, died of tuberculosis in 1847, at the age of twenty-four.

from *Seven Odes to Seven Natural Processes* (p. 126)

These three odes are from a group of seven written March–April 1984 as the centerpiece of *Facing Nature* (1985). As Updike states in that collection's jacket copy, together these seven odes are "a lyrical yet literal-minded celebration of some of the earthly forces that uphold and surround us," including—besides rot, growth, and healing—evaporation, fragmentation, entropy, and crystallization.

Ode to Rot: Completed March 1984. Published in *The Atlantic* 255:1 (January 1985), p. 83. Reprinted, as the first of "Seven Odes to Seven Natural Processes," in *Facing Nature* (1985), pp. 77–78, and *Collected Poems* (1993), pp. 191–93.

Updike's note in *Collected Poems* explains that the question "how / would . . . / the woodchuck corpse / vanish to leave behind a poem?" is an allusion to "Richard Eberhart's most celebrated poem, 'The Groundhog' [1934]."

Ode to Growth: Completed March 1984. Published in *Michigan Quarterly Review* 23:4 (Fall 1984), pp. 485–86. Reprinted, as the third of "Seven Odes to Seven Natural Processes," in *Facing Nature* (1985), pp. 82–83, and *Collected Poems* (1993), pp. 195–97.

Updike's note in *Collected Poems* explains that the phrase "linear growth comes to an end" (line 35) is a quotation from the article "Growth" in the *Encyclopædia Britannica*, 1969 edition.

Ode to Healing: Completed April 1984. Published in *Michigan Quarterly Review* 23:4 (Fall 1984), pp. 483–84. Reprinted, as the seventh of "Seven Odes to Seven Natural Processes," in *Facing Nature* (1985), pp. 90–92, and *Collected Poems* (1993), pp. 202–4.

Updike's note in *Collected Poems* explains that line 31—"the slings and arrows," "the thousand natural shocks"—consists of two quotations from *Hamlet* II.ii.

Munich (p. 131)

Completed April 23, 1985. Published in *The New Republic* 194:16 (April 21, 1986), p. 38. Reprinted in *Collected Poems* (1993), p. 205.

A Pear Like a Potato (p. 132)

Completed September 25, 1985. Published in *The New Yorker* 61:48 (January 20, 1986), p. 26. Reprinted in *Collected Poems* (1993), pp. 205–6.

Airport (p. 134)

Completed January 23, 1986. Published in *Ontario Review* 25 (Fall/Winter 1986/87), p. 23. Reprinted in *Collected Poems* (1993), p. 207.

Oxford, Thirty Years After (p. 135)

Completed April 1, 1986. Published in *The New Yorker* 62:22 (July 21, 1986), p. 32. Reprinted in *Collected Poems* (1993), p. 208.

In the spring of 1986, Updike visited Oxford for the first time since 1954–55, the year he was a scholarship student at the Ruskin School of Drawing and Fine Art.

Lines 1–6, "emperors' heads": Thirteen herms, or pillars topped with sculpted busts, are arranged in a rough semicircle around the rear entrance to Oxford's Sheldonian Theatre. The herms, a feature of the Sheldonian since it opened in 1668, have twice been copied and replaced. The third and present set, described here, were created in 1970–72 by the Oxford sculptor Michael Black.

Klimt and Schiele Confront the Cunt (p. 136)

Completed August 15, 1986. Published in *The Paris Review* 106 (Spring 1988), p. 203. Reprinted in *Collected Poems* (1993), p. 210.

Written after seeing the exhibition *Vienne: Naissance d'un siècle, 1880–1938*, on view at the Centre Georges Pompidou, Paris, from February 13 to May 15, 1986.

Line 19: Updike found Adele Astaire's epithet for the pubic patch in "Did You See the Ace of Spades?," a poem in Gavin Ewart's collection *The Young Pobble's Guide to His Toes* (London: Hutchinson, 1985).

Returning Native (p. 137)

Completed November 17, 1986. Published in *The New Republic* 197:5 (August 3, 1987), p. 33. Reprinted in *Collected Poems* (1993), pp. 211–12.

Updike's note in *Collected Poems* explains that greenbrier (genus *Smilax,* line 13) "is also called catbrier, for its 'anxious small claws.' "

Squirrels Mating (p. 139)

Completed October 25, 1987. Published in *The Atlantic* 264:1 (July 1989), p. 60. Reprinted in *Collected Poems* (1993), pp. 214–15.

Sails on All Saints' Day (p. 140)

Completed November 3, 1987. Published in *Shenandoah* 38:2 (Summer 1988), p. 40. Reprinted in *Collected Poems* (1993), pp. 215–16.

Tulsa (p. 141)

Completed November 7, 1987. Published in *Ontario Review* 29 (Fall/Winter 1988/89), p. 18. Reprinted in *Collected Poems* (1993), p. 216.

In Memoriam Felis Felis (p. 142)

Completed July 12, 1988. Published in *Grand Street* 8:4 (Summer 1989), pp. 137–38. Reprinted in *Collected Poems* (1993), pp. 220–21.

Updike's note in *Collected Poems* glosses "spice" (line 37) as "a bit of poetic license . . . conceived as the plural of 'spouse.' "

Enemies of a House (p. 144)

Completed August 6, 1988. Published in *The Southern California Anthology* 7 (1989), p. 15. Reprinted in *Collected Poems* (1993), p. 222.

Condo Moon (p. 145)

Completed August 8, 1988. Published in *The New Yorker* 64:41 (November 28, 1988), p. 44. Reprinted in *Collected Poems* (1993), p. 223.

The Beautiful Bowel Movement (p. 146)

Completed February 13, 1989. Published in *Oxford American* 1 (Spring 1992), p. 30. Reprinted in *Collected Poems* (1993), p. 224.

To a Box Turtle (p. 147)

Completed May 23, 1989. Published in *The New Yorker* 65:30 (September 11, 1989), p. 38. Reprinted in *Collected Poems* (1993), pp. 226–27.

Fall (p. 148)

Completed October 20, 1989. Published in *The American Poetry Review* 21:2 (March/April 1992), p. 35. Reprinted in *Collected Poems* (1993), p. 229.

Updike's mother, Linda Grace Hoyer Updike, died on October 10, 1989.

Perfection Wasted (p. 149)

Completed January 24, 1990. Published in *The New Yorker* 66:12 (May 7, 1990), p. 42. Reprinted in *Collected Poems* (1993), p. 231.

Working Outdoors in Winter (p. 150)

Completed January 26, 1990. Published in *The American Poetry Review* 21:2 (March/April 1992), p. 35. Reprinted in *Collected Poems* (1993), p. 232.

Granite (p. 151)

Completed September 14, 1990. Published in *The New Yorker* 66:38 (November 5, 1990), p. 48. Reprinted in *Collected Poems* (1993), pp. 238–39.

November (p. 152)

Completed November 7, 1990. Published in *The Formalist* 2:1 (Spring/Summer 1991), p. 46. Reprinted in *Collected Poems* (1993), p. 241.

Fly (p. 153)

Completed February 6, 1991. Published in *The Paris Review* 120 (Fall 1991), p. 41. Reprinted in *Collected Poems* (1993), pp. 243–44.

Updike's note in *Collected Poems* reads: "Written in the winter of 1991, during the heavy-bombing phase of the Gulf War."

Bindweed (p. 155)

Completed June 4, 1991. Published in *The New Yorker* 67:27 (August 26, 1991), p. 28. Reprinted in *Collected Poems* (1993), p. 245.

July (p. 156)

Completed July 7, 1991. Published in *The New Yorker* 68:22 (July 20, 1992), p. 30. Reprinted in *Collected Poems* (1993), pp. 245–46.

Updike's note in *Collected Poems* reads: "Perhaps these lines [4–12] make full sense only to those few of us who remember the summer baseball games at the Shillington playground field in the Thirties and Forties, with soft drinks being sold for a nickel from a zinc-lined cooler there in the shade of the wild cherry trees. The trees were not shapely and Japanese but tall and scraggly; children climbed them. The bolder they were, the higher they went, the girls rewarding timid boys on the ground with a glimpse of their underpants."

To a Dead Flame (p. 157)

Completed August 21, 1991. Published, as "To a Former Mistress, Now Dead," in *Poetry* 160:4 (July 1992), p. 201. Reprinted, under the present title, in *Collected Poems* (1993), pp. 246–48.

Elderly Sex (p. 159)

Completed December 26, 1991. Published in *Poetry* 160:4 (July 1992), p. 203. Reprinted in *Collected Poems* (1993), p. 249.

Academy (p. 160)

Completed May 11, 1992. Published in *Ontario Review* 38 (Spring/Summer 1993), p. 46. Reprinted in *Collected Poems* (1993), p. 254.

The academy of the title refers to both the 250-member American Academy of Arts and Letters and the academy's building at 633 West 155th Street, New York City.

Not Cancelled Yet (p. 161)

Completed March 21, 1993. Published in *Poetry* 164:5 (August 1994), p. 261. Reprinted as the final poem in *Not Cancelled Yet*, by John Updike (Boise: Limberlost Press, 2003), n.p., a chapbook of thirteen poems limited to seven hundred copies, one hundred of them signed by the author, and, posthumously, in Updike's nonfiction collection *Higher Gossip* (New York: Knopf, 2011), p. 51. The text from *Higher Gossip* is used here.

Downtime (p. 162)

Completed April 30, 1993. Published, as "Down Time," in *Poetry* 164:5 (August 1994), p. 259. Reprinted in *Americana* (2001), p. 46.

In the Cemetery High Above Shillington (p. 163)

Completed July 23, 1993. Published in *Ontario Review* 40 (Spring/Summer 1994), pp. 25–29. Reprinted in *Americana* (2001), pp. 29–34.

After this poem was published in *Americana*, Updike received a letter from an old Shillington acquaintance, Jerry Potts, providing and correcting details about Updike's former neighbors Gordon and Mamie Lutz. Updike rewrote the section of the poem introducing the Lutzes, expanding it from three lines to eleven, and tucked the insert into his office copy of the book. These revised lines (104–15) are printed here for the first time.

61 and Some (p. 169)

Completed August 27, 1993. Published, as "61 and 2/3," in *Poetry* 164:5 (August 1994), p. 261. Reprinted in *Americana* (2001), p. 35.

Americana (p. 170)

Completed December 2, 1993. Printed, as "Poem Begun on Thursday, October 14, 1993, at O'Hare Airport, Terminal 1, around Six O'Clock P.M.," both as a broadside and as a pamphlet, each in an edition of 126 copies signed by the author (Louisville, Kentucky: The Literary Renaissance, 1994). Reprinted in *Americana* (2001), pp. 3–5.

A Wound Posthumously Inflicted (p. 173)

Completed August 26, 1994. Published in *Ontario Review* 44 (Spring/Summer 1996), pp. 67–68. Reprinted in *Americana* (2001), pp. 38–39.

"Kit" is Christopher Lasch, the author of *The Culture of Narcissism* (1979) and a longtime professor of history at the University of Rochester. He died on February 14, 1994, at the age of sixty-one. The "posthumous book" (line 3) is *The Revolt of the Elites and the Betrayal of Democracy*, published in January 1995 by W. W. Norton.

Venetian Candy (p. 175)

Completed October 8, 1994. Published in *Poetry* 169:3 (January 1997), pp. 189–90. Reprinted in *Americana* (2001), pp. 62–63.

Two Cunts in Paris (p. 177)

Completed October 20, 1995. Published in *The Paris Review* 144 (Fall 1997), p. 166. Reprinted in *Americana* (2001), pp. 56–57.

L'Origine du monde (The Origin of the World), an oil on canvas by Gustave Courbet (1819–77), was painted in 1866, and *La Gimblette (Ring-Biscuit,* or *Little Pastry),* by Claude Michel (1738–1814), known as Clodion, was sculpted, in terra-cotta, circa 1800.

"Ici!": French for "Here!" or "Here I am!"

One Tough Keratosis (p. 179)

Completed April 6, 1996. Published in *Poetry* 169:3 (January 1997), p. 191. Reprinted in *Americana* (2001), pp. 41–42.

The Witnesses (p. 181)

Completed September 13, 1996. Published in *Ontario Review* 46 (Spring/Summer 1997), p. 73. Reprinted in *Americana* (2001), p. 53.

The Pinkas Synagogue (built c. 1535), now part of the Jewish Museum in Prague, was in 1955–60 repurposed as a museum commemorating the victims of the Holocaust from Bohemia and Moravia. On display on the first floor is a permanent installation of drawings by the children incarcerated by the Nazis at the Theresienstadt transit camp, also known as the Terezín ghetto, in 1942–44. In the words of the Jewish Museum's website, these drawings "document the transports to Terezín and daily life in the ghetto, as well as [the children's] dreams of returning home and of life in the Jewish homeland of Palestine. The vast majority of the children perished in the gas chambers of Auschwitz-Birkenau."

Icarus (p. 182)

Completed January 26, 1997. Published in *Partisan Review* 67:2 (Spring 2000), pp. 319–20. Reprinted in *Americana* (2001), pp. 14–15.

Upon Becoming a Senior Citizen (p. 184)

Completed March 24, 1997. Published in *The New Yorker* 73:16 (June 16, 1997), p. 84. Reprinted in *Americana* (2001), p. 37.

A Rescue (p. 185)

Completed July 21, 1997. Published in *Poetry* 174:3 (June 1999), p. 155. Reprinted in *Americana* (2001), p. 81.

Jacopo Pontormo (p. 186)

Completed July 21, 1997. Published in *Ontario Review* 48 (Spring/Summer 1998), p. 60. Reprinted in *Americana* (2001), p. 61.

The phrases in quotation marks are freely adapted from Vasari's life of Pontormo as translated into English, in 1912, by Gaston du C. De Vere.

Updike's footnotes to the poem, written in blank verse and published in both *Ontario Review* and *Americana*, read as follows:

Line 12, "He worked alone": "But for Bronzino, whom he seemed to love."

Lines 12–13, "His brain / 'strayed into vagaries.'": "According to Vasari's life, which speaks / of 'fantasies and cogitations' and / 'striving beyond his strength and forcing nature' / and 'wanting measure' in his final works. / How *fauve*, how modern were the Mannerists!"

Jesus and Elvis (p. 187)

Completed August 18, 1997. Published in *The New Yorker* 75:37 (December 6, 1999), p. 54. Reprinted in *Americana* (2001), p. 92.

Line 5, *"Talitha, cumi":* Mark 5:41, translated in the King James Version as "Damsel, I say unto thee, arise."

Replacing Sash Cords (p. 188)

Completed September 2, 1997. Published in *DoubleTake* 12 (Spring 1998), p. 120. Reprinted in *Americana* (2001), p. 82.

The Hedge (p. 189)

Completed October 4, 1997. Published in *The New Yorker* 75:14 (June 7, 1999), p. 74. Reprinted in *Americana* (2001), p. 28.

Song of Myself (p. 190)

Completed December 31, 1997. Published in *The Georgia Review* 52:2 (Summer 1998), pp. 265–68. Reprinted in *Americana* (2001), pp. 75–79.

To a Skylark (p. 194)

Completed June 3, 1998. Published in *The American Scholar* 68:2 (Spring 1999), p. 42. Reprinted in *Americana* (2001), p. 49.

Religious Consolation (p. 195)

Completed February 19, 1999. Published in *The New Republic* 221:8 (August 23, 1999), p. 43. Reprinted in *Americana* (2001), p. 93.

Line 13, "Moroni": According to Joseph Smith, prophet of the Church of Jesus Christ of Latter-day Saints, Moroni is the angel who presented him the golden plates on which the Book of Mormon was inscribed.

Saying Goodbye to Very Young Children (p. 196)

Completed August 2, 1999. Published in *Poetry* 176:2 (May 2000), p. 92. Reprinted in *Americana* (2001), p. 94.

A Sound Heard Early on the Morning of Christ's Nativity (p. 197)

Completed January 7, 2000. Published in *The Paris Review* 155 (Summer 2000), p. 139. Reprinted in *Americana* (2001), p. 95.

Boca Grande Sunset (p. 198)

Completed March 5, 2000. Published in *The American Scholar* 69:4 (Autumn 2000), p. 78. Reprinted in *Americana* (2001), p. 71.

Reality (p. 199)

Completed June 26, 2000. Published in *Ontario Review* 54 (Spring/Summer 2001), p. 101. Reprinted in *Americana* (2001), p. 45.

Chicory (p. 200)

Completed July 5, 2000. Published in *Ontario Review* 54 (Spring/Summer 2001), p. 100. Reprinted in *Americana* (2001), p. 91.

Rainbow (p. 201)

Completed July 17, 2000. Published in *The Atlantic* 286:5 (November 2000), p. 91. Reprinted in *Americana* (2001), p. 90.

Shinto (p. 202)

Completed October 27, 2000. Published in *The Yale Review* 89:2 (April 2001), p. 22. Reprinted in *Americana* (2001), p. 66.

December Sun (p. 203)

Completed December 7, 2000. Published in *Americana* (2001), p. 80.

Big Bard (p. 204)

Completed June 25, 2001. Published in *The American Scholar* 70:4 (Autumn 2001), p. 40, the source of the text used here.

Line 10, "Burbage": Richard Burbage (1568–1619) created the roles of Hamlet, Othello, Richard III, and Lear, among others.

Line 12, "Kempe and Armin": William Kempe (d. 1603) and Richard Armin (c. 1563–1615) created many of Shakespeare's comic roles.

Line 17, "(to quote Ben Jonson)": Jonson's words are from "De Shakespeare Nostrat," in his posthumous volume *Timber, or Discoveries Made upon Men and Matter* (1640).

Line 22: The American Harold Bloom (b. 1930) and the Canadian Northrop Frye (1912–1991) were two of the leading literary critics of Updike's twentieth century.

Waco (p. 205)

Completed November 14, 2001. Published in *Oxford American* 42 (Winter 2002), p. 60. Reprinted in *Endpoint* (2009), p. 61.

Lines 2–3: The Waco Suspension Bridge, designed and built by the Roebling's Sons Company, of Trenton, New Jersey, was opened in 1869, fourteen years before the completion of the Brooklyn Bridge.

Lines 8–14: The siege by U.S. government agents of the Branch Davidian compound at Mount Carmel Center, Texas, which lasted from February 28 to April 19, 1993, resulted in the death of four agents and eighty-two Branch Davidians, including the religious group's leader, thirty-three-year-old David Koresh.

Tools (p. 206)

Completed August 8, 2002. Published in *Poetry* 182:3 (June 2003), p. 134. Reprinted in *Endpoint* (2009), p. 79.

Stolen (p. 207)

Completed August 16, 2002, on the occasion of William Maxwell's ninety-fourth birthday. Published in *The New Yorker* 79:8 (April 14, 2003), p. 66. Reprinted in *A William Maxwell Portrait: Memories and Appreciations*, edited by Charles Baxter, Michael Collier, and Edward Hirsch (New York: Norton, 2004), pp. 17–18, and *Endpoint* (2009), pp. 33–34.

Maxwell, who edited Updike's fiction at *The New Yorker* from 1958 to 1976, died on July 31, 2000, at the age of ninety-one. The Gardner heist occurred just after midnight on March 18, 1990, Updike's fifty-eighth birthday.

Evening Concert, Sainte-Chapelle (p. 208)

Completed October 16, 2002. Published in *The New Yorker* 79:17 (June 30, 2003), p. 45. Reprinted in *Endpoint* (2009), p. 65.

Elegy for a Real Golfer (p. 209)

Completed July 4, 2003. Published in *Van Gogh's Ear* 3 (2004), p. 188, and *The American Poetry Review* 34:1 (January/February 2005), p. 15. Reprinted in *Endpoint* (2009), p. 39.

Payne Stewart died on October 25, 1999, at the age of forty-two.

Bird Caught in My Deer Netting (p. 210)

Completed January 5, 2004. Published in *The American Poetry Review* 34:1 (January/February 2005), p. 15. Reprinted in *Endpoint* (2009), p. 53.

Saguaros (p. 211)

Completed April 12, 2004. Published in *The New Yorker* 81:3 (March 7, 2005), p. 66. Reprinted in *Endpoint* (2009), p. 62.

Outliving One's Father (p. 212)

Completed August 25, 2004. Published in *Literary Imagination* 7:1 (Winter 2005), pp. 13–14. Reprinted in *Endpoint* (2009), p. 54.

Death of a Computer (p. 213)

Completed November 21, 2004. Published in *Van Gogh's Ear* 5 (2006), p. 228. Reprinted in *Endpoint* (2009), p. 47.

The computer is the IBM PS/2 that Updike used daily throughout the 1990s.

Lucian Freud (p. 214)

Written September 2005. Published in *The New York Review of Books* 53:9 (May 25, 2006), p. 23. Reprinted in *Endpoint* (2009), p. 72.

Lucian Freud, an exhibit of some ninety works by the artist spanning more than fifty years, was on view at the Museo Correr, Venice, from June 11 to October 30, 2005.

Line 9, "Saint-Gaudens' slim Diana": Copper statue (1892–93) by the American sculptor Augustus Saint-Gaudens (1848–1907), commissioned as a thirteen-foot weathervane for the tower of the second Madison Square Garden (1890–1925) but also existing in a series of later, half-sized bronzes. It depicts the Roman huntress as a fit young athlete—nude, balanced on her left foot, drawing back her bow.

Vacation Place (p. 215)

Completed April 8, 2006. Published in *Ontario Review* 66 (Spring/Summer 2007), p. 23. Reprinted in *Endpoint* (2009), p. 80.

The place was a casita in Tucson, Arizona.

Doo-Wop (p. 216)

Completed December 12, 2006. Published in *The Atlantic* 300:4 (November 2007), p. 64. Reprinted in *Endpoint* (2009), p. 36.

Frankie Laine (p. 217)

Completed February 25, 2007. Published in *The New York Review of Books* 54:9 (May 31, 2007), p. 8. Reprinted in *Endpoint* (2009), p. 35.

Laine died on February 6, 2007.

Baseball (p. 218)

Completed September 13, 2007, having been commissioned in August 2007 by J. E. Pitts, poetry editor of *Oxford American*, for a special sports issue of the quarterly. Published in *Oxford American* 59 (Winter 2007), p. 83. Reprinted in *Endpoint* (2009), pp. 40–41.

Her Coy Lover Sings Out (p. 220)

Completed April 29, 2008. Published, posthumously, in *Endpoint* (2009), pp. 37–38.

In *Endpoint*, Updike provided a footnote to line 2, "a mere twenty-one": "*Doris Day: The Untold Story of the Girl Next Door*, by David Kaufman (Virgin Books, 2008), has her born in the year 1922 (page 4), but her autobiography, *Doris Day: Her Own Story* (with A. E. Hotchner; Morrow, 1976), says she was born in 1924 (page 18). I have chosen, in this poem, to stick with the old chronology, as something I have grown used to." (Updike's *New Yorker* review of the Day/Hotchner book was collected in *Hugging the Shore* [1983], pp. 791–801.)

The epigraph is from "Can This Be Doris Day?" by Diane White (*Boston Globe*, January 8, 1976), which incorporates quotes from page 269 of the Day/Hotchner book.

Line 21: Molly Haskell (b. 1939) has served as film critic for *The Village Voice*, *New York*, and *Vogue*. Her profile of Day, whom she interviewed for *Ms.* magazine in 1975, was published, as "An Icon of the Fifties," in *Holding My Own in No Man's Land* (New York: Oxford University Press, 1997), pp. 21–34.

Line 32, "*Cara*": Italian for "Dear" or "Darling"—an endearment perhaps inspired by Doris Day's theme song, *"Que Sera, Sera."*

Endpoint (p. 222)

Written March 2002–December 2008. Submitted December 31, 2008, to Judith Jones, of Alfred A. Knopf, Inc., as part of the manuscript of *Endpoint and Other Poems*. Published in *Endpoint* (2009), pp. 3–29. The last ten poems in the sequence, all written in 2008, were published posthumously, under the collective title "Endpoint," in *The New Yorker* 85:5 (March 16, 2009), pp. 92–95. (Of the ten, only "Creeper" had been accepted by the magazine before Updike's death. The others were submitted to *The New Yorker* by Knopf in February 2009.) The seven earlier poems in the sequence were published individually, as detailed below.

March Birthday 2002, and After: Completed March 27, 2002. Published, as "March Birthday, and After," in *The New Yorker* 78:22 (August 5, 2002), pp. 62–63. Reprinted in *Endpoint* (2009), pp. 3–5.

03/18/03: Completed March 19, 2003. Printed as the tenth poem in *Not Cancelled Yet*, by John Updike (Boise: Limberlost Press, 2003), n.p., a chapbook of thirteen poems limited to seven hundred copies, one hundred of them signed by the author. Reprinted in *Endpoint* (2009), pp. 5–6.

Tucson Birthday, 2004: Completed April 12, 2004. Published, as "Tucson Birthday," in *The American Scholar* 73:4 (Autumn 2004), pp. 44–45. Reprinted in *Endpoint* (2009), pp. 7–8.

Line 16, "Crane Beach": In Ipswich, Massachusetts.

The Author Observes His Birthday, 2005: Completed May 7, 2005. Published, as "The

Author Observes His Birthday," in *Ontario Review* 64 (Spring/Summer 2006), pp. 33–36. Reprinted in *Endpoint* (2009), pp. 8–12.

Line 32: Lane Cooper (1875–1959) was an American literary scholar and a translator of Aristotle and Plato. As professor of English and classics at Cornell University (1902–43) he had a strong influence on the literary ideas of Updike's mother, who was his student in 1923–25.

Line 43: *The Poorhouse Fair* was Updike's first novel, published in 1959.

Line 44: Harry Ford (1918–1999) was a book and jacket designer at Knopf (1947–59, 1987–99) and Atheneum (1959–87) as well as a poetry editor. He established the "series look" of Updike's Knopf hardcovers, choosing Janson as the characteristic Updike typeface.

Line 50, "Blanche and Alfred": Mrs. and Mr. Alfred A. Knopf.

Line 52, "Bill Maxwell": See the note for "Stolen" (p. 207), above.

Line 60: Eustace Tilley is the top-hatted, monocled mascot of *The New Yorker.*

Line 78: Katharine S. White (1892–1977) was head of the fiction department at *The New Yorker* from 1925 to 1960. She accepted and edited Updike's earliest contributions to the magazine in fiction, humor, and poetry.

Line 80: Judith Jones (b. 1924) joined the firm of Alfred A. Knopf in 1957 and edited Updike's books from 1960 until his death.

Line 89, "Mr. Shawn": William Shawn (1907–1992), editor of *The New Yorker* from 1952 to 1987.

Line 93: Howard Moss (1922–1987) was poetry editor of *The New Yorker* from 1950 until his death. He edited Updike's poetry after Katharine S. White left New York for Maine in 1958.

My Mother at Her Desk: Completed May 30, 2006. Published in *The American Poetry Review* 37:6 (November/December 2008), p. 56. Reprinted in *Endpoint* (2009), pp. 12–13.

Dry Spell, 2006: Completed April 8, 2006. Published, as "Dry Spell," in *The American Poetry Review* 35:5 (September/October 2006), p. 68. Reprinted in *Endpoint* (2009), pp. 14–15.

Birthday Shopping, 2007: Completed May 4, 2007. Posted, as "Birthday Shopping," as part of the online quarterly *Per Contra* 10 (Spring 2008), www.percontra.net. Reprinted in *Endpoint* (2009), pp. 15–18.

Line 29, "Pomeroy's Department Store": In downtown Reading, Pennsylvania.

Spirit of 76: Completed April 18, 2008. Published, posthumously, in *The New Yorker* 85:5 (March 16, 2009), p. 93, and *Endpoint* (2009), pp. 18–20.

The occasion of the poem is the author's seventy-sixth birthday, which he celebrated in Tucson.

A Lightened Life: Completed, as "04/14/08," on April 14, 2008. Published, posthumously, in *The New Yorker* 85:5 (March 16, 2009), p. 93, and *Endpoint* (2009), pp. 20–21.

Line 1, "novel proofs": For *The Widows of Eastwick* (2008).

Line 7, "last novel's mild success": *Terrorist* (2006) spent four weeks on the *New York Times* Best Seller list, peaking at number five.

Euonymus 11/02/08: Completed November 2, 2008. Published, posthumously, in *The New Yorker* 85:5 (March 16, 2009), p. 94, and *Endpoint* (2009), p. 21.

Oblong Ghosts 11/06/08: Completed November 7, 2008. Published, posthumously, in *The New Yorker* 85:5 (March 16, 2009), p. 94, and in *Endpoint* (2009), pp. 21–22.

Lines 9–10: Barack Obama was elected the forty-fourth president of the United States on November 4, 2008, two days previous to the events of this poem.

Hospital 11/23–27/08: Completed December 3, 2008. Published, posthumously, in *The New Yorker* 85:5 (March 16, 2009), p. 94, and *Endpoint* (2009), pp. 22–24.

The City Outside 12/11/08: Completed December 12, 2008. Published, posthumously, in *The New Yorker* 85:5 (March 16, 2009), p. 95, and *Endpoint* (2009), pp. 24–26.

Peggy Lutz, Fred Muth 12/13/08: Completed December 13, 2008. Published, posthumously, in *The New Yorker* 85:5 (March 16, 2009), p. 95, and *Endpoint* (2009), pp. 26–27.

Needle Biopsy 12/22/08: Completed December 22, 2008. Published, posthumously, in *The New Yorker* 85:5 (March 16, 2009), p. 96, and *Endpoint* (2009), pp. 27–28.

Line 9, "All would be well . . . all manner of thing": Cf. the final stanza of T. S. Eliot's *Little Gidding* (1942), the last of the Four Quartets.

Creeper: Completed August 18, 2008. Published, posthumously, in *The New Yorker* 85:5 (March 16, 2009), p. 96, and *Endpoint* (2009), p. 28.

Fine Point 12/22/08: Completed December 22, 2008. Published, posthumously, in *The New Yorker* 85:5 (March 16, 2009), p. 96, and *Endpoint* (2009), p. 29.

Lines 12–14, *Surely . . . / goodness and mercy shall follow me all / the days of my life:* Psalms 23:6.

This volume presents the texts of the printings chosen for inclusion, as detailed above. The texts are presented without change, except for the corrections of typographical and stylistic errors, revisions made by the author in his office copies of *Collected Poems* and *Americana*, and, in two instances, variants adopted by the editor. ("Stylistic errors" are departures from Updike's preferred book style, which adhered closely to that of *The New Yorker.* This style employs, among other features, double "l"s, "p"s, and "t"s that are otherwise moribund in American orthography—"cancelled," "worshipped," "benefitted," and the like—and the chiefly British ending "-re," in words such as "ochre" and "spectre." Most of these stylistic errors are found in the posthumous *Endpoint*, the proofs of which did not enjoy the benefit of the author's reading.)

The following is a list of typographical and stylistic errors corrected, cited by page and line number (line numbers include titles and subheadings but not stanza breaks): 32.3, "Tilley" (for "Tilly"); 86.19, "Cold War" (for "Cold-War"); 206.14, "meagre" (for "meager"); 207.18, "benefitted?" (for "benefited?"); 211.8, "sombre" (for "somber"); 213.7, "bejewelled" (for "bejeweled"); 214.11, "Saint-Gaudens'" (for "Saint-Gaudens's"); 220.21, "year?)," (for "year?)"); 227.28, "Blondie," (for "*Blondie*,"); 229.12, "channelled" (for "channeled"); 233.23–24, "screens. / [stanza break] / Hi-def" (for "prepare / [stanza break] / our"); 236.13, "quarrelling" (for "quarreling"); 236.15, "76" (for "'76"); 238.2, "04/14/08" (for "4/14/08"); 239.1, "11/06/08" (for "11/6/08");

240.4, "years)," (for "years)"); 240.17, "first wife's" (for "first-wife's"); 240.22, "goodbye" (for "good-bye"); 253.29, "Siege-bread." (for "Seige-bread.").

The following is a list of revisions made by the author: 23.2–3, "Playing golf on Cape Ann in October, / I saw something to remember." (stanza restored from text in *Telephone Poles*); 23.12, "and around." (for "from golf.", words restored from text in *Telephone Poles*); 24.18–19, "Long had it been since my heart / had been lifted as it was by the lifting of that great scarf." (stanza restored from text in *Telephone Poles*); 88.12–13, "first proclaimed / *Mu*SHROOM! just" (for "after all / Went *mu*SHROOM!"); 109.15, "gave" (for "lent"); 113.22, "through the" (for "through"); 165.30–166.4, "lie. Across the street // . . . // the Reading *Eagle* featured in its news." (for "lie, MARIE and BILL, / who used to sit upon their well-used porch / and nod toward our less fertile domicile."); 166.12, "visible in her complacent" (for "precious, set visible in her"); 169.6, "brown" (for "tan"); 170.3, "1, Concourse B, around" (for "3, around"); 186.15, "dead belief." (for "disbelief."); 203.15, "clock that ticks until we" (for "clockwork guts that make us").

The following variants were adopted by the editor: 8.2–3, "(*Having Taken Along to the Ball Game / Arthur Waley's* Three Ways of Thought in Ancient China)" (from the text in the 1982 edition of *The Carpentered Hen*); 223.28, "death-day" (for "death day," from the texts in *The New Yorker* and the 2003 chapbook *Not Cancelled Yet*).

Short Chronology

1932 Born John Hoyer Updike on March 18 in Reading Hospital, West Reading, Pennsylvania, the only child of Wesley Russell Updike (b. 1900), a former telephone lineman collecting credits toward a state teaching certificate, and Linda Grace Hoyer Updike (b. 1904), an as yet unpublished writer of fiction. (Parents met in 1919, when both were students at Ursinus College, and married in 1925, after Linda Hoyer earned a master's degree in English from Cornell University.) The family lives in Shillington (pop. 4,400), three miles southwest of Reading, at 117 Philadelphia Avenue, the home of Linda's parents, John Franklin Hoyer (b. 1863), a retired farmer who had lost his fortune in the crash of 1929, and Katherine Ziemer Kramer Hoyer (b. 1873), a farmwife made prematurely frail by Parkinson's disease.

1937 Enters kindergarten at Shillington Elementary School, which he will attend through grade six. Shows a talent for drawing that his mother encourages.

1938 Onset of psoriasis, followed by a stutter, both of which will prove lifelong afflictions. In fall begins Sunday school at Grace Evangelical Lutheran Church, where his father is a deacon.

1939 Keeps scrapbooks of comic strips from the Reading *Times* and *Eagle*, and copies the drawings to learn the artists' techniques. Fascinated by Mickey Mouse cartoons, he aspires to become an animator for Walt Disney, an ambition he will entertain until his late teens.

1942 Takes lessons in drawing and painting from neighbor Clint Shilling, a commercial artist and a conservator at the Reading art museum.

1943 For Christmas receives a gift subscription to *The New Yorker* from his father's sister, Aunt Mary Updike, and is captivated by the magazine's cartoons, light verse, humor pieces, design, and tone. New York and *The New Yorker* become, in his phrase, "the object of my fantasies and aspirations."

1944 Enters seventh grade at Shillington High School, where his father is a math teacher.

1945 Joins the staff of the *Chatterbox*, the high school's mimeographed student weekly, to which he will contribute hundreds of drawings, poems, and movie reviews over the next five years. In October the family—he, his parents, and his maternal grandparents—move to Plowville, in Robeson Township, eleven miles south of Shillington. Their home, known as Strawberry Hill, is the unimproved sandstone farmhouse (built 1812) where his grandparents once lived and where his mother was born.

1950 Graduates from Shillington High School as co-valedictorian. Types his collected poems, 1941–50, and has the sheets professionally bound into a unique hardcover volume titled *Up to Graduation*. Spends the first of three consecutive summers as a copyboy for the Reading *Eagle*, which publishes some of his light verse in its weekly humor column. In September enrolls in Harvard College, which has awarded him a full-tuition scholarship.

1951 In spring is elected to *The Harvard Lampoon* and quickly distinguishes himself as the monthly magazine's most prolific and versatile staff member, a contributor of short stories, poems, and light verse as well as cartoons, spot drawings, and cover illustrations. Dates Radcliffe undergraduate Mary Pennington, a fine-arts major two years his senior.

1953 On June 26 marries Mary Pennington, and the newlyweds honeymoon in Ipswich, Massachusetts, on the North Shore of greater Boston. Serves as president and editor-in-chief of the *Lampoon* for 1953–54. Submits undergraduate poems and short fiction to *The New Yorker* and receives letters of encouragement from editors William Maxwell and Katharine S. White. Grandfather Hoyer dies at the age of ninety.

1954 Graduates from Harvard *summa cum laude* and is awarded a scholarship for one year's study at the Ruskin School of Drawing and Fine Art, in Oxford, England. In June *The New Yorker* accepts "Duet, with Muffled Brake Drums," an item of light verse published in the issue for August 14. ("From this poem's acceptance," Updike will later write, "I date my life as a professional writer.") By the end of the summer Katharine S. White purchases two more poems and the short story "Friends from Philadelphia." In September signs a contract with *The New Yorker* granting the editors first-reading rights in his work.

1955 Daughter, Elizabeth, born April 1. In June Katharine S. White and her husband, E. B. White, then touring the U.K., visit Updike in Oxford to offer him a position at *The New Yorker*. In July takes an apartment at Riverside Drive and West Eighty-fifth Street and in August starts at the magazine as a writer for "The Talk of the Town." Grandmother Hoyer dies at the age of eighty-three.

1956 Devotes mornings and weekends to writing "Home," a novel (never published) based on his Shillington boyhood. Writes "Snowing in Greenwich Village," the first of more than a dozen stories chronicling the increasingly difficult marriage of his characters Joan and Richard Maple.

1957 Son, David, born January 19. One week later Updike resolves to quit his job at *The New Yorker* and to support his family as freelancer in Ipswich, Massachusetts. Rents a small house for one year, beginning April 1, and there completes a draft of his novel. Sends it and a collection of poems to Cass Canfield, publisher of Harper & Row, who rejects "Home" but accepts the poems. Regularly attends Clifton Lutheran Church, in Marblehead, Massachusetts. Discovers an aptitude for golf, a game that becomes a lifelong passion.

1958 First book, the collection of poems *The Carpentered Hen* (U.K. title: *Hoping for a Hoopoe*), published. Purchases a seventeenth-century house at 26 East Street, Ipswich, which will be his home for the next twelve years.

1959 First novel, *The Poorhouse Fair*, and a collection of stories, *The Same Door*, published by Alfred A. Knopf, his chief publisher for the rest of his life. With Mary joins the First Congregational Church in Ipswich. Third child, Michael, born May 14.

1960 In September attends Ted Williams's final game at Fenway Park and writes first-person account of it, "Hub Fans Bid Kid Adieu," for *The New Yorker*. In November second novel, *Rabbit, Run*, published to good reviews and strong sales. Fourth child, Miranda, born December 15.

1961 Mother publishes a short story in *The New Yorker* under her maiden name, Linda Grace Hoyer. (Over the next two decades she will contribute nine more stories to the magazine and write two novels published by Houghton Mifflin.) In September Updike writes the first of nearly four hundred signed book reviews for *The New Yorker*.

1962 *Pigeon Feathers and Other Stories* published.

1963 Third novel, *The Centaur*, published, followed by *Telephone Poles and Other Poems*.

1964 Writes "Marry Me," a novel based closely on his adulterous affair with an Ipswich neighbor, but chooses not to publish it. *The Centaur* wins the National Book Award for fiction. Updike is elected, at the age of thirty-two, to the National Institute of Arts and Letters. Enjoys a six-week trip as American cultural ambassador to the Soviet Union with fellow writer John Cheever. *Olinger Stories: A Selection* published in paperback by Vintage Books.

1965 *Assorted Prose*, a collection of essays and criticism, published, followed by the short novel *Of the Farm*. "The Bulgarian Poetess," the first of twenty stories concerning the fictional Jewish American writer Henry Bech, appears in *The New Yorker*. *A Child's Calendar*, twelve poems for young readers, published.

1966 *The Music School*, a third collection of stories, published. Donates his literary manuscripts, 1953–66, to Houghton Library, Harvard University. (Harvard will purchase the rest of his papers shortly after his death, in 2009.)

1967 Experiments with theater, accepting commissions for a historical pageant from the town of Ipswich and the libretto for a children's opera from the Opera Company of Boston. Resolves to write a closet drama about the life and death of President James Buchanan.

1968 In April the novel *Couples* begins a yearlong run near the top of the *New York Times* Best Seller list and occasions a cover story on Updike in *Time* magazine. In the summer he and his family escape celebrity by renting a flat in London for the 1968–69 school year.

1969 *Midpoint*, a third collection of poems, published.

1970 Purchases a larger house at 50 Labor-in-Vain Road, Ipswich. Sells his previous residence to a Boston-based lawyer, Alexander Bernhard, and his wife, Martha Ruggles Bernhard, who soon become part of the Updikes' social circle. Publishes *Bech: A Book*, a collection of seven linked short stories.

1971 *Rabbit Redux*, a sequel to *Rabbit, Run*, published.

1972 *Museums and Women and Other Stories* published. Father dies, April 16, at the age of seventy-two.

1973 Delivers Phi Beta Kappa poem at Harvard University. Writes a personal essay on golf for *The New York Times*, and is soon in demand as a commentator on the game by *Golf Digest* and other sports publications.

1974 Updike and Martha Bernhard, their four-year acquaintance having developed into a deep attachment, decide to leave their spouses for each other. Updike leases "bachelor's accommodations" in Boston's Back Bay neighborhood, which he will keep for twenty months while his and Martha's divorces are finalized. Publishes his closet drama, *Buchanan Dying.*

1975 Novel *A Month of Sundays* published, followed by a second collection of essays and criticism, *Picked-Up Pieces.*

1976 Purchases house at 58 West Main Street, Georgetown, Massachusetts, ten miles west of Ipswich. In June is joined there by Martha and her three sons, John (twelve), Jason (eleven), and Ted (five). *Marry Me*, a novel tabled for nearly twelve years, published.

1977 *Tossing and Turning*, a fourth collection of poems, published. On September 30 marries Martha Bernhard at Clifton Lutheran Church.

1978 Novel *The Coup* published.

1979 *Too Far to Go* (U.K. title: *Your Lover Just Called*), an omnibus of stories about Richard and Joan Maple, published in paperback by Fawcett. It is followed in the fall by *Problems and Other Stories.* Writes a series of brief essays on painting and sculpture for *Réalités* magazine, his first foray into art criticism.

1981 Publishes *Rabbit Is Rich*, a third novel exploring the life and times of his recurring protagonist Harry "Rabbit" Angstrom. In the following year it will win a Pulitzer Prize, a National Book Critics Circle Award, and an American Book Award.

1982 Purchases house at 675 Hale Street, Beverly Farms, Massachusetts, twenty miles southeast of Georgetown, which will be his home for the rest of his life. Like Martha becomes a parishioner at local St. John's Episcopal Church. Publishes *Bech Is Back*, a second collection of Bech stories. In October *Time* magazine publishes "Going Great at 50," a second cover story about Updike and his work.

1983 Publishes *Hugging the Shore,* a third collection of essays and criticism. Confirmed in the Episcopal Church by the Bishop of Massachusetts.

1984 *Hugging the Shore* wins a National Book Critics Circle Award. Novel *The Witches of Eastwick* published. Edits annual *Best American Short Stories* collection, published by Houghton Mifflin.

1985 *Facing Nature*, a fifth collection of poems, published.

1986 Novel *Roger's Version* published.

1987 *Trust Me*, a collection of short stories, published.

1988 Novel *S.* published.

1989 *Self-Consciousness*, a volume of memoirs, published. With the appearance of *Just Looking: Essays on Art* is invited to write exhibition reviews for *The New York Review of Books*. (He will contribute sixty pieces on the visual arts to the magazine over the next two decades.) Mother dies, October 10, at the age of eighty-five.

1990 *Rabbit at Rest*, the fourth and final novel about "Rabbit" Angstrom, published. The following spring it will win a Pulitzer Prize and a National Book Critics Circle Award.

1991 *Odd Jobs*, a fourth collection of essays and criticism, published.

1992 Novel *Memories of the Ford Administration* published.

1993 *Collected Poems 1953–1993* published.

1994 Novel *Brazil* published, followed by *The Afterlife and Other Stories.*

1995 *Rabbit Angstrom*, an omnibus edition of the four Rabbit novels, published by Everyman's Library. *Rabbit at Rest* awarded the William Dean Howells Medal of the American Academy of Arts and Letters for the most distinguished work of fiction of the last five years. *A Helpful Alphabet of Friendly Objects*, a book of light verse for young readers, published.

1996 Novel *In the Beauty of the Lilies* published, followed by *Golf Dreams: Writings on Golf.*

1997 Novel *Toward the End of Time* published.

1998 *Bech at Bay*, a third Bech collection, published. Edits *A Century of Arts and Letters*, a history of the American Academy of Arts and Letters published by Columbia University Press.

1999 *More Matter*, a fifth collection of essays and criticism, published. Edits *The Best American Short Stories of the Century*, published by Houghton Mifflin.

2000 Novel *Gertrude and Claudius* published. It is followed by *Licks of Love*, a collection of twelve short stories and a novella, "Rabbit Remembered."

2001 *The Complete Henry Bech*, an omnibus collection of Bech stories, published by Everyman's Library. It is followed by *Americana*, his seventh collection of poems.

2002 Novel *Seek My Face* published.

2003 Omnibus *The Early Stories: 1953–1975* published.

2004 Novel *Villages* published.

2005 *Still Looking*, a second collection of illustrated art essays, published.

2006 Novel *Terrorist* published.

2007 Awarded the Gold Medal in Fiction by the American Academy of Arts and Letters. *Due Considerations*, a sixth collection of essays and criticism, published.

2008 Delivers the manuscript of *The Maples Stories*, an expanded edition of *Too Far to Go* solicited by Everyman's Library. Compiles *My Father's Tears*, a collection of recent short stories. *The Widows of Eastwick*, a sequel to *The Witches of Eastwick*, published. In November believes that he is suffering from pneumonia but is diagnosed as having stage IV lung cancer. Keeps a journal in verse of his visits to Massachusetts General Hospital and prepares the manuscript of a final book, *Endpoint and Other Poems.*

2009 On January 2, files his last piece for *The New Yorker*, a review of Blake Bailey's life of John Cheever. Dies in hospice, January 27, in Danvers, Massachusetts, at the age of seventy-six. He is cremated, and his ashes are buried privately. *Endpoint*, *My Father's Tears*, and *The Maples Stories* published posthumously. In July 2010, his children place a memorial headstone for him near the graves of his parents and grandparents in Plow Cemetery, in Plowville, Pennsylvania.

Index of Titles

Date indicates year of completion, when the poem was submitted for publication

A NOTE ABOUT THE EDITOR

Christopher Carduff is a member of the staff of The Library of America and the editor of John Updike's posthumous volumes *Higher Gossip*, *Always Looking,* and *The Collected Stories*. He lives in Melrose, Massachusetts.

A NOTE ABOUT BRAD LEITHAUSER

Brad Leithauser is the author of sixteen books, the most recent of which is *The Oldest Word for Dawn: New and Selected Poems.* The recipient of a MacArthur Fellowship and Iceland's Order of the Falcon, he is a professor in the Writing Seminars at Johns Hopkins University and divides his time between Baltimore, Maryland, and Amherst, Massachusetts.

A NOTE ON THE TYPE

This book was set in Baskerville, a facsimile of the type cast from the original matrices designed by John Baskerville. The original face was the forerunner of the modern group of typefaces.

Composed by North Market Street Graphics,
Lancaster, Pennsylvania

Printed and bound by Thomson-Shore,
Dexter, Michigan